The New Improved Big6™ Workshop Handbook

D1611579

By Mike Eisenberg & Bob Berkowitz

This book was provided to your library
through funding from:
The Superiorland Preview Center
Mary Ann Paulin, Director
1615 Presque Isle Ave., Marquette, MI
49855 (906) 228-7697
The Library Services and Technology Act
The publisher and/or distributor
and the following reviewer(s):

Linworth Publishing, Inc.
Worthington, Ohio

Curric
025.5
E4

Published by Linworth Publishing, Inc.
480 East Wilson Bridge Road, Suite L
Worthington, Ohio 43085-2372

Copyright © 1999 Michael B. Eisenberg and Robert E. Berkowitz

All rights reserved. Reproduction of this book in whole or in part, print or electronic, without permission of the authors, is prohibited except for not-for-profit educational use in the classroom, in the school library, in professional workshops sponsored by elementary and secondary schools, or other similar not-for-profit activities.

ISBN 0-938865-87-0

5 4 3 2 1

OLSON LIBRARY
NORTHERN MICHIGAN UNIVERSITY
MARQUETTE, MICHIGAN 49855

The New Improved Big6™ Workshop Handbook

Contents

The New Improved Big6™ Workbook Handbook

Contents (continued)

Foreword

Hello Big6ers present and future!

We are very pleased to provide you with *The New Improved Big6™ Workshop Handbook.* It really is "new and improved."

Our previous handbook was used as part of a professional development workshop guided by one of us. This new publication still fills that need, but it is also designed as a stand-alone handbook to help educators learn the Big6 and to help teach the Big6 to other educators, parents, and community members. To accomplish this, we have added new worksheets and resources as well as explanations on how we use the various materials in Big6 training contexts. All together, *The Handbook* focuses on learning about, using, and teaching the Big6 Skills approach to information and technology skills.

Information and technology literacy is a major concern throughout our society in education, in business, and in our personal lives. There is widespread recognition that basic life skills for the 21st century are related to the use of information and technology. All people need the ability to identify information needs and then find, use, apply, and evaluate information for those needs. That's what the Big6 is all about.

At its most fundamental level, the Big6 is a process model for information problem-solving. We have worked with thousands of students—pre-K through higher education—as well as people in business, government, and communities to improve their information and technology skills.

The Big6 represents much more than just the process itself. We have worked with educators in the U.S. and around the world to systematically implement the Big6 in classrooms, library programs, and communities. Therefore, the Big6 stands for practical implementation of information and technology skills programs through integrating Big6 Skills in subject area curriculum. The Big6 is an approach to learning and teaching information and technology skills in meaningful contexts.

Finally, because of the widespread use of the Big6 (it is the most extensively used information literacy model in the world) and the various resources and services surrounding the Big6 (e.g., *The Big6 Newsletter*, books, articles, posters, cards, bookmarks, videos, the Big6 listserv, and Big6 website), those involved with the Big6 are really part of a "movement." This Big6 movement is dedicated to helping people learn essential information and technology skills for success.

The New Improved Big6™ Workshop Handbook addresses all these views of the Big6. It is intended to help classroom teachers, teacher-librarians, technology teachers, administrators, parents, community members, and students to do the following:

- Learn about the Big6
- Use the Big6 process in their own activities, and
- Implement a Big6 information and technology skills program in classrooms, libraries, and labs; in individual schools and districts; in regions and states; and even as part of national and international initiatives.

The New Improved Big6™ Workshop Handbook is especially designed as a collection of workshop materials for continuing professional education programs. It contains tried and tested exercises, activities, and information that help participants learn the process, approach, and power of the Big6.

Part I and Part II of the book help the reader identify the need for information and technology skills and develops a working understanding of the Big6. Part III focuses on technology and how to use technology in a meaningful way through integration within the Big6 framework. Part IV turns to implementing the Big6—on the micro (lesson and unit) level. Part V offers specific approaches to assessment using the Big6 steps, and Part VI shows the importance of collaboration and partnerships. Part VII prepares readers to integrate Big6 Skills with the curriculum by using curriculum-mapping techniques. The final sections of the book, Part VIII and Part IX, provide exercises for including parents and the school district (macro level) in the overall plan for success.

If you are just beginning to use the Big6, this book will be a good resource of information about the Big6 approach and how it can be implemented in your school. If you are already using the Big6, this book will provide additional understandings and will help you to expand your efforts. In addition, *The New Improved Big6™ Workshop Handbook* may be used to support local Big6 professional education initiatives. A number of colleagues plan to purchase multiple copies to conduct their own Big6 training events. So—THINK BIG! What we do in terms of education and teaching essential information and technology skills is critically important to student success in school and in later life. These skills are not optional—they are basic skills for the 21st century. We hope this *Workshop Handbook* helps you make the Big6 an effective information and technology literacy program in your educational setting.

We would like to thank some amazing people—Beth Mahoney, Carrie Lowe, and Sue Wurster for their help, encouragement, and special skills that made this book a reality. And to our publisher, Marlene Woo-Lun, a truly unique and supportive person—it is a great pleasure to work with you.

Mike Eisenberg & Bob Berkowitz
Seattle, Washington and Rochester, New York
May 14, 1999

Part I:

Introducing the Big6™

Introduction

Number Connecting Exercise

The Information Age: Implications for Learning & Teaching

Information Literacy: The Big6 Skills Process & Approach

Introduction

All journeys begin with a first step. In some respects, taking that first step forward takes a certain degree of courage—especially when setting out on a new road. A new road represents change. Change. It is an idea that excites but at the same time can make us quite uncomfortable.

In his workshops, Mike often starts with a Calvin and Hobbes cartoon about change. It's the one that shows Calvin and Hobbes coming down a hill in a wagon. Calvin says, "I thrive on change." Hobbes says, "You? You threw a fit this morning because your mom put less jelly on your toast than yesterday." Calvin then says, "I thrive on making *other* people change."

Education today is all about change. There are all kinds of new demands on teachers and students—some driven by environment and mandates, but the more profound demands are created by fundamental changes in our society—the information society. We live in an increasingly complex information world. Education—schools, teachers, caregivers—must come to grips with what knowledge and skills students really need and then make sure that students gain the needed knowledge and skills.

We can no longer rely on the old ways of doing things—a textbook, lecture, and test. Instead, we need to use a wide range of resources, guide and assist, and assess through a range of individual and collaborative projects. The information society demands that students need to find, use, and process a wide range of information, often in a very short period of time. Students learn these skills through guidance, teamwork, and projects. And, we assess their skills and knowledge by looking at the authentic results of their efforts.

Making these changes will not necessarily be easy, but it is vital that we do so. The materials in this chapter can help. The chapter is designed help you understand the nature of instructional change, how to overcome resistance to it, and how to approach others to make changes with you.

The first activity in the *Workshop Handbook*—the Number Connecting Exercise—is designed to address people's natural aversion to change. As you and other participants go through this exercise, it becomes evident that shifts of focus or process are okay—healthy and appropriate. Several elements must be in place in order to effect change. These elements include the following:

- Compatibility: Compatible with current instructional practice
- Complexity: Easy to understand and explain to others
- Observability: Observable as change
- Try-ability: Easy to try without taking a big risk.

CCOT – that's one way to remember these aspects of creating change – CCOT.

Despite the complex look of this first activity, it satisfies the CCOT principles of change. Numbers, number recognition, and number sequencing are well-known skills among the vast majority of adults and children alike. Teachers often ask students to engage these kinds of skills (Compatibility). The exercise is simple to do even though there is a time constraint that adds to the challenge, and there are only two instructions (Complexity). The visual nature makes it easy for the participant to see what he or she has done, and whether the participant has changed his or her approach (Observability). All participants will feel comfortable trying this exercise; it minimizes risk factors that may inhibit a participant's willingness to engage in the task.

Potential risk factors include embarrassment, fear of failure, or lack of time. The participants do this activity on their own, and are not required to share the results thus eliminating the potential for embarrassment. There is no way for a participant to fail in the exercise because there are multiple opportunities to practice the skills, and each person will improve to some degree. Lastly, the activity takes only two and one-half to three minutes to complete which effectively eliminates the excuse that trying the exercise will take too long (Try-ability).

Bob uses the Number Connecting Exercise to make some key points about change:

1. Change: Be careful not to get too complacent, too comfortable. Change is just around the corner.

2. Repetition: We learn through repetition.

3. Patterns: There are patterns that we can learn to help us be effective and efficient.

4. Shared experiences: Sharing common experiences helps to bring people together.

The Number Connecting Exercise is our first introduction to change and the challenges facing students and educators. Following the Number Connecting exercise is a handout of *PowerPoint* slides used to present a discussion about the challenges of the information society. We all know that the amount of available information is overwhelming. Our experience is that most people need a system for "sorting and sifting" all of this information. They also want a successful method for becoming efficient and effective information problem solvers. That's the Big6.

The *PowerPoint* slides offer a context for the Big6 in terms of information literacy and information needs in our society. We also provide insights into the key role for library media specialists in ensuring that students gain the skills they need. Both of us come from a library media background. We are tireless supporters of an active, engaged role for teacher-librarians in collaborating with classroom teachers and others to provide meaningful, integrated Big6 instruction.

We expect you to supplement these *PowerPoint* slides with slides of your own. You will have numerous opportunities to personalize your Big6 presentation throughout this handbook, and we encourage you to do so. Think about the different audiences for the Big6, and how you would customize your presentation of the information. Also consider how you will evaluate whether you were successful so that you can improve for the next time.

In summary, this first section introduces change and a new approach to thinking about (1) the skills and knowledge that students really need, and (2) how to help students gain those skills and knowledge.

We believe that students must be effective and efficient information problem-solvers, and that we must change our schools and ourselves in order to help students succeed.

Number Connecting Exercise

Directions

*Please do **not** open this packet until you are told to do so.*

This packet contains five sheets of numbers. The numbers are scattered all over the page, but they are all there and it will be your job to find them. To get you started, the number one will always be found at the top left corner; it has a circle around it.

Your job will be to connect, with a pen, the numbers in order, beginning with number one, then two, then three, and so on. You should work as fast as you can because your goal is to connect as many numbers as possible. However, please note that:

1. You must begin with the number one and you cannot skip any numbers. Thus, you cannot connect 30 to 31 until you have already connected the previous 29 numbers.

2. Lines can cross. When you are done, there will not be a picture of anything.

There are five pages of numbers. You will be allotted 30 seconds per page. On each page, **you must begin again with the number one.** Work as fast as you can. You will be told when your time is up.

① 53 39 15 16 54

27 51 28 40 6

13 17 5 2 26 62

29 3 41 38 14 50 30

37 49 25 18 4 42

7 23 31 55 46 36

35 43 22 12 34

11 19 57 44 24

47 33 45 8 20 32 58

21 9 59 48 60 10 56

1 53 39 15 16 54

27 51 28 40 6

13 17 5 2 26 62

3 41 14 50 30

29 38

37 49 25 18 4 42

7 23 31 55 46 36

35 43 22 12 34

11 19 57 44 24

47 33 45 8 32 20 58

21 9 59 48 60 10 56

1 53 39 15 16 54

27 51 28 40 6

13 17 5 2 26 52

3 41 14 50 30

29 38

37 49 25 18 4 42

7 23 31 55 46 36

35 43 22 12 34

11 19 57 44 24

8

47 33 45 20 32 58

21 9 59 48 60 10 56

(1) 53 39 15 16 54

27 51 28 40 6

62

5 2 26

13 17

3 41 14 50 30

29 38

37 49 25 18 4 42

7 23 55 46 36

31

35 43 22 12 34

11 19 57 44 24

8

47 33 45 20 32 58

21 9 59 48 60 10 56

(1) 33 9 25 23 45

49 41 37 59 13

19 35 15 21 29

51 3 27 7 55 47

11 31

43 57 17 53 39 5

34 12 20 36 56 22 46

18 2 40 54 8

50 28 58 14 30

38 48

42 26 44 6 24

4 10 52 32 60 16

The Information Age: Implications for Learning & Teaching

Information Literacy

"To be information literate, a person must be able to recognize when information is needed and have the ability to locate, evaluate, and use effectively the needed information."

- American Library Association, 1989

"Information literacy, the ability to locate, process and use information effectively, equips individuals to take advantage of the opportunities inherent in the global information society."

- Assoc. for Supervision & Curriculum Dev., 1991

Recognition of Need

U.S. Dept. of Labor (*Secretary's Commission on Achieving Necessary Skills [SCANS] Report*, 1991):

Competencies for all entry level employees:

- acquires and uses information
- works with a variety of technologies

Peter Drucker (*Wall Street Journal*, Dec. 1, 1992):

"Executives have become computer literate...but not many executives are information literate."

The Super3

You are the main character in a story:

Beginning - **Plan**

Middle - **Do**

End - **Review**

Information Literacy (The Big6 Skills)

1. Task Definition
2. Information Seeking Strategies
3. Location & Access
4. Use of Information
5. Synthesis
6. Evaluation

WANTED: In Business and Education

An information unit—staffed with information professionals—able to deal with the overwhelming quantity of information and the complexity of information systems. Able to <u>provide</u> direct information on demand; <u>consult</u> on appropriate uses of information technology; and <u>instruct</u> in information access, use, manipulation, and evaluation.

Key Players to Help Meet the Need: Library Media Specialists

"The mission of the library media program is to ensure that students...are effective users of ideas and information."

Information Power: Guidelines for School Library Media Programs, AASL and AECT, 1988.

Eisenberg & Berkowitz, 1998

The Big6™ Skills Approach to Information Problem-Solving

1. Task Definition

1.1 Define the problem.

1.2 Identify the information needed.

2. Information Seeking Strategies

2.1 Determine all possible sources.

2.2 Select the best source.

3. Location & Access

3.1 Locate sources.

3.2 Find information within sources.

4. Use of Information

4.1 Engage (e.g., read, hear, view).

4.2 Extract relevant information.

5. Synthesis

5.1 Organize information from multiple sources.

5.2 Present the result.

6. Evaluation

6.1 Judge the result (effectiveness).

6.2 Judge the process (efficiency).

© Eisenberg/Berkowitz, 1987

Think Sheet

Part II:

Learning the Big6™

Introduction

Information Literacy: The Big6 Skills Process & Approach

Developing Big6 Understandings: Worksheets

Introduction

In this part of the *Workshop Handbook*, we get to the heart of our approach to information and technology literacy: the Big6.

- Explanations of the Big6 at different levels and for different age groups
- A chart showing the Big6 in different contexts: school, life, and work, and
- Exercises that help develop a Big6 understanding.

The first set of materials explains the stages of the Big6—as a process and as individual sets of skills. The stages are important as part of the Big6 process. These are the necessary process stages for solving information problems and they represent a flow from beginning (figuring out what needs to be done) to middle (gathering and using necessary information) to end (creating a resulting product and evaluating success). Successful information problem-solving requires successfully completing each of these stages, however this does not necessarily follow in a step-by-step fashion. For example, sometimes we jump from Task Definition—figuring out the scope of a project—to Synthesis—creating an outline of what the result might look like. Then, we might loop back and determine the resources we wish to use (Information Seeking Strategies) and so on. Similarly, Evaluation—determining effectiveness and efficiency—is not only an ending skill but Evaluation occurs as students engage in every Big6 stage. Students are constantly jumping from stages in the process to Evaluation and back.

We suggest spending some time reviewing the language of the Big6—the formal statements describing the stages in the process, the detailed explanations for each Big6 Skill, and the Big6 stages as questions for elementary level children.

The charts that follow present the Big6 in the context of specific settings: school, life, and work. One of the strengths of the Big6 is its wide applicability across situations and settings. We firmly believe in making learning relevant. Students constantly question the applicability of what they learn in school. That's easy with the Big6. The Big6 Skills that children learn at school are applicable to their lives beyond school. If they become effective and efficient information problem-solvers in school, they will be effective and efficient information problem-solvers beyond school.

In addition to the chart with the three examples (an assignment for class, selecting a movie, and creating a work report), we provide a blank chart so you can brainstorm school-home-work situations from the audience. Have them work through each one according to the Big6—in small groups or with the entire audience.

At first glance, the Big6 often seems like common sense. "It's simple," some say—and on one level it is. However, the Big6 also encompasses some complex critical thinking abilities. We provide a set of worksheets to help develop Big6 understandings and to gain an appreciation of the nuances of skills at each stage.

The exercises take you through literal, interpretive, and applied levels of understanding. For example, Worksheet one requires identification of the Big6 Skill(s) students are using when engaging in twelve different activities. This is a literal level application of the information that was previously presented. The next set of worksheets requires an interpretive response. Completing the worksheets requires application of knowledge by explaining the skills to be taught and the explanation of choices. The last group of worksheets is open-ended, providing a structure for developing more independence in order to apply understandings of the Big6 process and skills.

We are all information consumers—in school, work, and life settings. In order to put our students in a position to be effective consumers as well, we must provide them with the tools for understanding the nature of information and using information throughout their lives. The Big6 provides a framework for teaching them this most important lesson.

Working through this chapter increases competence in understanding the Big6 process and the depth of thinking and skills required in each Big6 stage.

Information Literacy: The Big6™ Skills Process & Approach

Big6 #1
Task Definition
The student demonstrates the ability to:

- Determine the information problem to be solved
- Reformulate a complete statement of the task
- Pick out key words embedded in a question
- Ask a good question
- Understand and follow printed and/or oral directions.

Big6 #2
Information Seeking Strategies
The student demonstrates the ability to:

- Develop alternatives and to seek a variety of materials
- Determine which information is most/ least important
- Recognize that information can be gathered from many sources, including investigation, observation, and human resources
- Use appropriate criteria for selecting sources.

Big6 #3
Location & Access
The student demonstrates the ability to:

- Determine what sources are available
- Independently gather resources
- Determine if the source is usable
- Access appropriate information systems, including: online databases, union catalog, electronic multimedia.

© Eisenberg/Berkowitz, 1987

Information Literacy: The Big6™ Skills Process & Approach

Big6 #4
Use of Information
The student demonstrates the ability to:

- Distinguish facts from opinion
- Accurately and completely summarize/paraphrase the main idea from written and oral sources
- Accurately cite sources
- Read, listen, view, and touch carefully to acquire information.

Big6 #5
Synthesis
The student demonstrates the ability to:

- Organize information in clear, coherent presentations
- Present information in ways appropriate to the task
- Participate effectively in discussions and debates
- Produce personally designed products to communicate content.

Big6 #6
Evaluation
The student demonstrates the ability to:

- Demonstrate a high degree of confidence in the quality of the product produced
- Assess the product for completeness, strengths, and weaknesses
- Develop criteria to determine the effectiveness of the process used to solve the problem
- Provide recommendations to improve results
- Determine the need for further information.

© Eisenberg/Berkowitz, 1987

Information Literacy: The Big6™ Skills Process & Approach

Information Literacy: The Big6™ Skills Process & Approach
Information Problem-Solving in School, Life, and Work Contexts

Information Problem-Solving Process	School Context: Completing an assignment for class	Life Context: Deciding which movie to attend on Saturday night	Work Context: Reporting on five years products sales
Task Definition	Finding out that the task involves writing a two-part essay and realizing that a key to success is using documented supporting evidence.	Figuring out that it will be necessary to attend a 7:00-7:30 p.m. showing in order to get the babysitter home on time.	Producing a readable chart representing sales figures by product and salesperson. Determining that reliable sales data by department will be needed.
Information Seeking Strategies	Considering all potential information sources and deciding that current journals and newspapers would be best.	Deciding to look at the entertainment section of the newspaper to determine the showing times of movies.	Determining that there are two places where sales figures are kept: on paper and on computer disks. Deciding to use the computer version.
Location & Access	Using an online index to search for appropriate periodical articles. Finding the articles online and in print.	Locating the newspaper upstairs next to the bed. Using the "Quick Guide" on the first page to locate the entertainment section.	Finding disks with the sales data and identifying the relevant files.
Use of Information	Reading the articles and typing notes directly into a word processing program, noting the sources.	Reading the movie ads and focusing on times and locations.	Examining the various files, cutting and pasting the data by relevant categories and years.
Synthesis	Using a word processor, creating an outline, then a draft of the essay.	Determining that there is only one movie playing at the time that you both want to see.	Using an electronic spreadsheet program to combine the various sales data and generating a chart from the spreadsheet.
Evaluation	Realizing that your details are weak on one of the two parts and that you need to go back and find additional information.	Realizing that the newspaper was a good source for the necessary information and that you successfully met your task.	Being congratulated by your manager for a nice job; recognizing that the spreadsheet software was more than adequate for the task.

Information Literacy: The Big6™ Skills Process & Approach
Information Problem-Solving in School, Life, and Work Contexts

Information Problem-Solving Process	School Context	Life Context	Work Context
Task Definition			
Information Seeking Strategies			
Location & Access			
Use of Information			
Synthesis			
Evaluation			

Developing Big6™ Understandings: Worksheet 2-1—Literal Level

In the space provided, indicate which of the Big6 Skills students are using when they perform each of the following activities:

TD = Task Definition
ISS = Information Seeking Strategies
L&A = Location & Access
UI = Use of Information
S = Synthesis
E = Evaluation

When a student

_____ 1. chooses between an encyclopedia and a magazine for information on the political situation in the Middle East.

_____ 2. creates a weekly classroom newsletter about freedom movements in the world.

_____ 3. interviews a long-time community resident about local history.

_____ 4. assesses the presentations of other students.

_____ 5. uses *Hyperstudio* to create a multimedia show about holiday celebrations in other cultures.

_____ 6. reflects on personal information skills that need improving.

_____ 7. learns and uses appropriate Yahoo or Alta Vista commands.

_____ 8. evaluates the effectiveness of different specific media (e.g. political ads, car commercials, video vs. audio, etc.)

_____ 9. writes a thesis statement.

_____ 10. identifies two ways to find words in a dictionary.

_____ 11. answers questions using a textbook.

_____ 12. selects a specific topic for a science fair project.

Developing Big6™ Understandings: Worksheet 2-2—Interpretive Level

Curriculum Context: For homework, Sally must answer questions at the end of a chapter in her science textbook.

Student Activities	Big6	Explanation
Sally decides that she will need to use her science book to answer the questions.		
Sally writes the answers to the questions, noting the page numbers(s) where she found the answers.		
Sally thinks about how she used the bold headings to locate the answers and realizes it was a helpful technique.		
Sally calls her friend Tanya about the assignment. Tanya reminds Sally to write the answers in complete sentences.		
Sally reads a section looking for the answer to question four.		
Sally uses the bold headings to get to the section that seems to be the right one for question four.		

The Big6 Skills © 1987 Eisenberg & Berkowitz

Task Definition

1.1 Define the problem.

1.2 Identify the information needed.

Information Seeking Strategies

2.1 Determine all possible sources.

2.2 Select the best sources.

Location & Access

3.1 Locate sources.

3.2 Find information within sources.

Use of Information

4.1 Engage (e.g., read, hear, view).

4.2 Extract relevant information.

Synthesis

5.1 Organize info from multiple sources.

5.2 Present the result.

Evaluation

6.1 Judge the result (effectiveness).

6.2 Judge the process (efficiency).

NMU LIBRARY

Developing Big6™ Understandings: Worksheet 2-3—Interpretive Level

Curriculum Context: Middle school students are working on interdisciplinary group projects on regions of the U.S. including cultural, geological, social, geographic, and historical aspects.

Student Activities	Big6	Explanation
Group three uses the online catalog to find books while group four is using the periodical index.		
The groups brainstorm possible sources of information and decide to use magazines, books, their parents, and the WWW.		
The students discuss which Web sites were useful and why.		
Group four prints out a magazine article.		
Each student group selects an area of the U.S. as the focus of their report.		
Group five delivers their report in the form of a TV news show.		

The Big6 Skills © 1987 Eisenberg & Berkowitz

Task Definition
- 1.1 Define the problem.
- 1.2 Identify the information needed.

Information Seeking Strategies
- 2.1 Determine all possible sources.
- 2.2 Select the best sources.

Location & Access
- 3.1 Locate sources.
- 3.2 Find information within sources.

Use of Information
- 4.1 Engage (e.g., read, hear, view).
- 4.2 Extract relevant information.

Synthesis
- 5.1 Organize info from multiple sources.
- 5.2 Present the result.

Evaluation
- 6.1 Judge the result (effectiveness).
- 6.2 Judge the process (efficiency).

Developing Big6™ Understandings: Worksheet 2-4—Interpretive Level

Curriculum Context: Joe, a 10th grade student, has just finished reading *The Call of the Wild.* As part of a take-home exam, he is required to write an essay comparing various aspects of his life to Buck's life.

Student Activities	Big6	Explanation
Joe marks appropriate sections in the book with paper clips then enters some relevant quotations in a word processing document.		
Joe realizes that he earned an A on his essay because he referred to specific examples in the book.		
Joe scans through the book to find the section where Buck first hears the "call of the wild."		
Joe realizes that the task involves writing a coherent and organized essay with specific comparisons between his life and Buck's life.		
Joe determines that it will be necessary to use a copy of the *Call of the Wild,* but a critical analysis would also help.		
Joe prepares a chart of events in his life and in Buck's life, then uses word-processing to write and print his essay.		

The Big6 Skills © 1987 Eisenberg & Berkowitz

Task Definition
- 1.1 Define the problem.
- 1.2 Identify the information needed.

Information Seeking Strategies
- 2.1 Determine all possible sources.
- 2.2 Select the best sources.

Location & Access
- 3.1 Locate sources.
- 3.2 Find information within sources.

Use of Information
- 4.1 Engage (e.g., read, hear, view).
- 4.2 Extract relevant information.

Synthesis
- 5.1 Organize info from multiple sources.
- 5.2 Present the result.

Evaluation
- 6.1 Judge the result (effectiveness).
- 6.2 Judge the process (efficiency).

Developing Big6™ Understandings: Worksheet 2-5—Interpretive Level

Curriculum Context: A 2nd grade class is studying animals that live in their area. Each student is to make a book that includes a picture of three animals and a very short story (a sentence or two) about each animal.

Student Activities	Big6	Explanation
The students and teacher brainstorm to identify some animals that live nearby. Students may use one from this list but must decide on two others on their own.		
The teacher debriefs with the class--what was the most difficult part of the assignment?		
The library media specialist helps the students find the books and magazines about animals in the library media center.		
The students decide that a visit to the local nature center would be very helpful.		
The library media specialist shows students how to write notes on index cards about their animals.		
Some students draw pictures of the animals with crayons or paint, while other students paste pictures from old magazines.		

The Big6 Skills © 1987 Eisenberg & Berkowitz

Task Definition
- 1.1 Define the problem.
- 1.2 Identify the information needed.

Information Seeking Strategies
- 2.1 Determine all possible sources.
- 2.2 Select the best sources.

Location & Access
- 3.1 Locate sources.
- 3.2 Find information within sources.

Use of Information
- 4.1 Engage (e.g., read, hear, view).
- 4.2 Extract relevant information.

Synthesis
- 5.1 Organize info from multiple sources.
- 5.2 Present the result.

Evaluation
- 6.1 Judge the result (effectiveness).
- 6.2 Judge the process (efficiency).

Developing Big6™ Understandings: Worksheet 2-6—Interpretive Level

Curriculum Context: Students in a 4th grade class are studying their family history. Each student is to construct a chart listing one significant family event and one significant U.S. historical event for each year of their life.

Student Activities	Big6	Explanation
Students decide that some possible sources for U.S. history information are: their textbooks, the CD-ROM references, and possibly the WWW.	**Task Definition**	
After trying to draw a chart by hand, a student uses a graphics program to construct the chart of her family events and U.S. historical events.	**Information Seeking Strategies**	
A student uses a microcassette recorder to tape an interview with her parents about the important events in her life.	**Location & Access**	
By comparing charts with each other, students decide they could prepare neater and more legible charts if they learned how to use computers.	**Use of Information**	
Students determine that the task will require them to use both personal and U.S. history information.	**Synthesis**	
A student uses Lycos to search for U.S. history information on the WWW.	**Evaluation**	

The Big6 Skills © 1987 Eisenberg & Berkowitz

Task Definition

1.1 Define the problem.

1.2 Identify the information needed.

Information Seeking Strategies

2.1 Determine all possible sources.

2.2 Select the best sources.

Location & Access

3.1 Locate sources.

3.2 Find information within sources.

Use of Information

4.1 Engage (e.g., read, hear, view).

4.2 Extract relevant information.

Synthesis

5.1 Organize info from multiple sources.

5.2 Present the result.

Evaluation

6.1 Judge the result (effectiveness).

6.2 Judge the process (efficiency).

Developing Big6™ Understandings: Worksheet 2-7—Interpretive Level

Curriculum Context: Students in 9th grade are given a vocabulary list of literary devices (e.g., metaphor, allusion, hyperbole, etc.) to define. The teacher requires that they rewrite the definitions in their own words and provide an example of each device.

Student Activities	Big6	Explanation
Students use the glossary in the back of the book.		
The teacher says that students can use a dictionary, or the glossary in the textbook.		
Each student assesses the amount of time that the assignment took.		
Students determine that to be successful they must write the definitions in their own words.		
Students make a word processed list of terms and definitions.		
A student takes notes from the dictionary before writing the definition in his own words.		

The Big6 Skills © 1987 Eisenberg & Berkowitz

Task Definition

1.1 Define the problem.

1.2 Identify the information needed.

Information Seeking Strategies

2.1 Determine all possible sources.

2.2 Select the best sources.

Location & Access

3.1 Locate sources.

3.2 Find information within sources.

Use of Information

4.1 Engage (e.g., read, hear, view).

4.2 Extract relevant information.

Synthesis

5.1 Organize info from multiple sources.

5.2 Present the result.

Evaluation

6.1 Judge the result (effectiveness).

6.2 Judge the process (efficiency).

Developing Big6™ Understandings: Worksheet 2-8—Interpretive Level

Curriculum Context: Students in a 4th grade music class are studying "note and rest values."

Student Activities	Big6	Explanation
One group creates a computer quiz in *Hyperstudio.*		
The class discusses which of the tests were hard and why.		
The teacher explains that they will be working in groups and the assignment is to make a test for others.		
The library media specialist directs the students to the music books.		
One group decides that they want some more information and they head to the library media center.		
Students photocopy pages from three books in the library media center.		

The Big6 Skills © 1987 Eisenberg & Berkowitz

Task Definition

1.1 Define the problem.

1.2 Identify the information needed.

Information Seeking Strategies

2.1 Determine all possible sources.

2.2 Select the best sources.

Location & Access

3.1 Locate sources.

3.2 Find information within sources.

Use of Information

4.1 Engage (e.g., read, hear, view).

4.2 Extract relevant information.

Synthesis

5.1 Organize info from multiple sources.

5.2 Present the result.

Evaluation

6.1 Judge the result (effectiveness).

6.2 Judge the process (efficiency).

Developing Big6™ Understandings: Worksheet 2-9—Applied Level

Describe one or two activities that relate to each of the Big6 Skills for the following curriculum content.

Curriculum Context: Students in a 1st grade class are studying nutrition and food groups. Students are required to make a poster that describes what they learned. Each poster should include examples of foods that belong in each food group. Additionally, each food group must be correctly labeled.

Big6	Student Activities

The Big6 Skills © 1987 Eisenberg & Berkowitz

Task Definition

1.1 Define the problem.

1.2 Identify the information needed.

Information Seeking Strategies

2.1 Determine all possible sources.

2.2 Select the best sources.

Location & Access

3.1 Locate sources.

3.2 Find information within sources.

Use of Information

4.1 Engage (e.g., read, hear, view).

4.2 Extract relevant information.

Synthesis

5.1 Organize info from multiple sources.

5.2 Present the result.

Evaluation

6.1 Judge the result (effectiveness).

6.2 Judge the process (efficiency).

Developing Big6™ Understandings: Worksheet 2-10—Applied Level

Describe one or two activities that relate to each of the Big6 Skills for the following curriculum content.

Curriculum Context: A 7th grade science class is studying rocks. Students are required to demonstrate their knowledge by preparing a special project that shows what they learned about the types of rocks and how they were formed.

Big6	Student Activities

The Big6 Skills © 1987 Eisenberg & Berkowitz

Task Definition

1.1 Define the problem.

1.2 Identify the information needed.

Information Seeking Strategies

2.1 Determine all possible sources.

2.2 Select the best sources.

Location & Access

3.1 Locate sources.

3.2 Find information within sources.

Use of Information

4.1 Engage (e.g., read, hear, view).

4.2 Extract relevant information.

Synthesis

5.1 Organize info from multiple sources.

5.2 Present the result.

Evaluation

6.1 Judge the result (effectiveness).

6.2 Judge the process (efficiency).

Developing Big6™ Understandings: Worksheet 2-11—Applied Level

Describe one or two activities that relate to each of the Big6 Skills for the following curriculum content.

Curriculum Context: Students in an 11th grade class are divided into small groups to study significant Supreme Court cases. Each group is assigned a specific case on which to report. Next, each group is required to prepare a three part project (oral, visual, and written products) to explain the background, the decision and the impact of the decision. When they are finished, each group will share their research with the rest of the class.

Big6	Student Activities

The Big6 Skills © 1987 Eisenberg & Berkowitz

Task Definition

1.1 Define the problem.

1.2 Identify the information needed.

Information Seeking Strategies

2.1 Determine all possible sources.

2.2 Select the best sources.

Location & Access

3.1 Locate sources.

3.2 Find information within sources.

Use of Information

4.1 Engage (e.g., read, hear, view).

4.2 Extract relevant information.

Synthesis

5.1 Organize info from multiple sources.

5.2 Present the result.

Evaluation

6.1 Judge the result (effectiveness).

6.2 Judge the process (efficiency).

Developing Big6™ Understandings: Worksheet 2-12

Curriculum Context: Create a typical, integrated curriculum situation. Describe one or two activities that relate to each of the Big6 Skills.

Big6 Skills	Activities
1. Task Definition 1.1 Define the problem. 1.2 Identify the information needed.	
2. Information Seeking Strategies 2.1 Determine all possible sources. 2.2 Select the best source.	
3. Location & Access 3.1 Locate sources. 3.2 Find information within sources.	
4. Use of Information 4.1 Engage (e.g., read, hear, view). 4.2 Extract relevant information.	
5. Synthesis 5.1 Organize information from multiple sources. 5.2 Present the result.	
6. Evaluation 6.1 Judge the result (effectiveness). 6.2 Judge the process (efficiency).	

Developing Big6™ Understandings: Worksheet 2-13

Curriculum Context: Create a typical, integrated curriculum situation. Describe one or two activities that relate to each of the Big6 Skills.

Big6 Skills	Activities
1. Task Definition 1.1 Define the problem. 1.2 Identify the information needed.	
2. Information Seeking Strategies 2.1 Determine all possible sources. 2.2 Select the best source.	
3. Location & Access 3.1 Locate sources. 3.2 Find information within sources.	
4. Use of Information 4.1 Engage (e.g., read, hear, view). 4.2 Extract relevant information.	
5. Synthesis 5.1 Organize information from multiple sources. 5.2 Present the result.	
6. Evaluation 6.1 Judge the result (effectiveness). 6.2 Judge the process (efficiency).	

Developing Big6™ Understandings: Worksheet 2-14

Curriculum Situations	Big6 Connection

Think Sheet

Part III:

Technology and the Big6™

Introduction

Technology and technology skills are integral to the Big6 process and approach. K-12 schools are finally moving away from teaching computer skills in isolation—as skills to be applied at a later time or in lab settings separate from the classroom. Students need to be able to use computers flexibly, creatively, and purposefully. Today, educators at all levels are seeking to move from teaching isolated computer skills to teaching integrated information and technology skills.

For us, that means integrating computer skills within the Big6 problem-solving process. Individual computer skills take on a new meaning when they are integrated within the Big6, and students develop true "computer literacy" because they have genuinely applied various computer and technology skills as part of the learning process. Considering technology within a Big6 context provides the necessary structure and framework for this to happen. Effective integration of information and technology skills learning has two requirements: (1) the skills must directly relate to the content area curriculum and to classroom assignments, and (2) the skills themselves need to be tied together in a logical and systematic information process model. The same trend is taking place in relation to teaching computer skills.

The first page in this section sets the technology context. The *PowerPoint* handout in this section displays the slides that Mike uses to present his thoughts on the current and immediate future state of technology. As noted in the introduction to Part I, we expect you to supplement these *PowerPoint* slides with slides of your own.

The next two worksheets are used in an exercise to demonstrate the relationship between technology and the Big6. Technology skills are easily integrated into the Big6 Skills model. The first column—baseline technologies—is used for non-electronic tools that students use. A crayon and paper, for example, is a baseline technology that can be entered into the top line in the first column. Now, what's the related Big6 Skill(s)? Where, in the Big6 does a crayon and paper prove valuable? The answer is Synthesis, and that can be entered into the second column. Finally, what are the related electronic technologies that provide a similar boost to crayon and paper, only more so? The answer should include such software as paint or draw, graphics programs, or even video editing. These can be entered into the third column.

Baseline Technologies	Related Big6 Skills	Related Electronic Technologies
• The yellow pages	• Location & Access	• Search tools/engines; indexes
• A highlighter	• Use of Information	• Copy and paste
• Books and magazines	• Information Seeking Strategies	• Full-text electronic resources
• A pen and paper	• Use of Information/Synthesis	• Word processing; desktop publishing; presentation software
• The telephone	• Location & Access	• E-mail
• A face-to-face meeting.	• Task Definition/Information Seeking Strategies, Location & Access, Use of Information, Synthesis, and Evaluation.	• E-mail, chat, audio or video conferencing.

After the exercise, the relationship can be turned around—using the next worksheet. That is, for each of the Big6 stages indicate the related electronic technologies. This chart forms the basis of the Big6-technology connection. For example, word processing, desktop publishing, *HyperStudio* and other presentation software programs are used for Synthesis (to organize and present). Word processing is also important for Use of Information (note-taking). Online databases, CD-ROM encyclopedias, and other electronic resources are part of an effective Information Seeking Strategy and provide Location & Access capabilities. Various Internet capabilities are also included in information problem-solving. E-mail is highly useful for linking students with their teachers or each other for Task Definition activities and later for Evaluation. Web browsers and search engines (e.g., Yahoo, Lycos, AltaVista) are used in Information Seeking Strategies and as tools for location and access. FTP and downloading/uploading help students to use information. When integrated into the information problem-solving process, these technological capabilities become powerful information tools for students.

The Big6-technology connection is further explained in the "Technology Within the Big6 Framework" chart and the reprinted ERIC Digest. The final chart, "Information Services—Including Technology" links various library media services to various technologies.

Technology: Today & Tomorrow

Global Networking

Search Engines node home pages Lynx file transfer JAVA WebCrawlers Middle_L LM_NET lynx download upload Usenet MOO telnet URL Alta Vista netnews HTML Web Lycos Yahoo protocol Browsers freenets gopher Netscape tcp/ip archie ftp ICONNECT/KidsConnect e-mail AskERIC Yahoo file server Listservs Explorer bitnet Infoseek SLIP K12ADMIN address

Other Technologies: Today

- **Processing Tools:** for words, numbers, sound, images, video, time, plans, ...any type of data or resource
- **Fully and Continually Connected Networks:** Local Area Networks, the Internet, Extranets, Network Computers (NCs)
- **Completely Integrated Systems:** offering a full range of resources and access tools through portals and common interfaces, on file servers, CD-ROM towers, juke boxes
- **Personal Assistants:** laptops, PDAs, PIMs, HPCs synchronized

Technologies: Today and...

- **Integrated**: across computer and communications platforms and systems, the Internet appliance; intranets; embedded
- **Multimedia**: well beyond current interactive multimedia and virtual reality computing environments; audio and video streaming
- **Live interactive, multimedia, connectivity**: Chat, text, audio, video, graphic , video conferencing, Internet telephone, groupware
- **Intelligent**: natural language understanding and voice recognition
- **Intelligent**: able to learn, individualize, customize; electronic agents, knowbots

The Technology & Internet Challenge

- To use technology and the Internet in meaningful ways to help achieve educational goals.
- To focus on the question:

What are we trying to accomplish—in terms of learning and teaching—and how can technology and the Internet help us to do so?

Technology as a Tool: Applications in a Big6 Context

Word processing, graphics, desktop publishing	Synthesis Use of Information
Information Retrieval and search systems	Info Seeking Strategies Location & Access
Spreadsheets, DBMS	Synthesis
Hypermedia	Use of Information Synthesis
Electronic resources (on CD-ROM, servers, WWW)	Info Seeking Strategies Location & Access

Technology as a Tool: Internet Applications in a Big6 Context

E-mail, listservs, Chat, video conferencing	Task Definition, Evaluation Info Seeking Strategies
Network navigation (WWW Netscape, I.E); portals	Info Seeking Strategies Location & Access
Ftp, download/upload	Use of Information
Yahoo, Lycos, Infoseek Alta vista, portals	Location & Access
Home page (WWW) development	Synthesis

Eisenberg & Berkowitz, 1998

Technology Within the Big6™ Framework

Baseline Technology	Related Big6 Skill(s)	Related Electronic Technologies

Technology Within the Big6™ Framework

Use	Technology	Notes
1. Task Definition 1.1 Define the problem. 1.2 Identify the information needed.		
2. Information Seeking Strategies 2.1 Determine all possible sources. 2.2 Select the best source.		
3. Location & Access 3.1 Locate sources. 3.2 Find information within sources.		
4. Use of Information 4.1 Engage (e.g., read, hear, view). 4.2 Extract relevant information.		
5. Synthesis 5.1 Organize information from multiple sources. 5.2 Present the result.		
6. Evaluation 6.1 Judge the result (effectiveness). 6.2 Judge the process (efficiency).		

Technology Within the Big6™ Framework

Use	
1. Task Definition 1.1 Define the problem. 1.2 Identify the information needed.	E-mail, online discussions (listservs, newsgroups), chat, video, conferencing (CUSeeMe), desktop conferencing, groupware, brainstorming software
2. Information Seeking Strategies 2.1 Determine all possible sources. 2.2 Select the best source.	Online catalogs, information retrieval, electronic resources (CD-ROMs nets), WWW/net resources, AskERIC, KidsConnect, online discussion groups (listservs, newsgroups)
3. Location & Access 3.1 Locate sources. 3.2 Find information within sources.	Online catalogs, electronic indexes, WWW navigation and search tools (Yahoo, Alta Vista, Lycos, WebCrawler), AskERIC, KidsConnect, telnet, ftp, e-mail
4. Use of Information 4.1 Engage (e.g., read, hear, view). 4.2 Extract relevant information.	Upload/download, word processing, cut-paste, outliners, spreadsheets, databases (for analysis of data), statistical packages
5. Synthesis 5.1 Organize information from multiple sources. 5.2 Present the result.	Word processing, desktop publishing, graphics, spreadsheets, database management, hypermedia, presentation software, down/up load, ftp e-journals, listservs, newsgroups, Web creation (HTML)
6. Evaluation 6.1 Judge the result (effectiveness). 6.2 Judge the process (efficiency).	Spell/grammar checkers, e-mail, online discussion (listservs, newsgroups), MOO, IRC, CUSeeMe, desktop conferencing, groupware

March 1996 EDO-IR-96-04

Computer Skills for Information Problem-Solving: Learning and Teaching Technology in Context

by Michael B. Eisenberg and Doug Johnson

There seems to be clear and widespread agreement among the public and educators that students need to be proficient computer users--students need to be "computer literate." However, while districts are spending a great deal of money on technology, there seems to be only a vague notion of what computer literacy really means.

- Can the student who operates a computer well enough to play Doom be considered computer literate?
- Will a student who has used computers in school only for running tutorials or an integrated learning system have the skills necessary to survive in our society?
- Will the ability to do basic word processing be sufficient for students entering the workplace or post-secondary education?

Clearly not. In too many schools, most teachers and students still use computers only as the equivalent of expensive flash cards or electronic worksheets. The productivity side of computer use in the general content area curriculum is neglected or grossly underdeveloped (Moursund, 1995).

There are, however, some encouraging signs concerning computers and technology in education. For example, it is becoming increasingly popular for educational technologists to advocate integrating computers into the content areas. Teachers and administrators are recognizing that computer skills should not be taught in isolation, and that separate "computer classes" do not really help students learn to apply computer skills in meaningful ways. This is an important shift in approach and emphasis. And it's a shift with which library media specialists have a great deal of familiarity.

Library media specialists know that moving from isolated skills instruction to an integrated approach is an important step that takes a great deal of planning and effort. Over the past 20 years, library media professionals have worked hard to move from teaching isolated "library skills" to teaching integrated information skills. Effective integration of information skills has two requirements:

1. The skills must directly relate to the content area curriculum and to classroom assignments, and
2. The skills themselves need to be tied together in a logical and systematic information process model.

Schools seeking to move from isolated computer skills instruction will also need to focus on both of these requirements. Successful integrated information skills programs are designed around collaborative projects jointly planned and taught by teachers and library media professionals. Computer skills instruction can follow the same approach. Library media specialists, computer teachers, and classroom teachers need to work together to develop units and lessons that will include both computer skills, general information skills, and content-area curriculum outcomes.

A meaningful, unified computer literacy curriculum must be more than "laundry lists" of isolated skills, such as:

- knowing the parts of the computer
- writing drafts and final products with a word processor
- searching for information using a CD-ROM database.

While these specific skills are certainly important for students to learn, the "laundry list" approach does not provide an adequate model for students to transfer and apply skills from situation to situation. These curricula address the "how" of computer use, but rarely the "when" or "why." Students may learn isolated skills and tools, but they will still lack an understanding of how those various skills fit together to solve problems and complete tasks. Students need to be able to use computers flexibly, creatively and purposefully. All learners should be able to recognize what they need to accomplish, determine whether a computer will help them to do so, and then be able to use the computer as part of the process of accomplishing their task. Individual computer skills take on a new meaning when they are integrated within this type of information problem-solving process, and students develop true "computer literacy" because they have genuinely applied various computer skills as part of the learning process.

The curriculum outlined below, "Computer Skills for Information Problem-Solving," demonstrates how computer literacy skills can fit within an information literacy skills context (American Association of School Librarians, 1995). The baseline information literacy context is the Big Six Skills process (see sidebar and Eisenberg & Berkowitz cites). The various computer skills are adapted from curricula developed by the state of Minnesota (Minnesota Department of Education, 1989) and the Mankato Area Public Schools (Mankato Schools Information Literacy Curriculum Guideline). These basic computer skills are those which all students might reasonably be expected to authentically demonstrate before graduation. Since Internet-related skills are increasingly important for information problem-solving, they are included in this curriculum, and are noted by an asterisk.

Some computer literacy "skills" competencies which do not seem to fit into this information processing model, and which may or may not be important to have stated include:

- knowing the basic operation, terminology, and maintenance of equipment
- knowing how to use computer-assisted instructional programs
- having knowledge of the impact of technology on careers, society, and culture
- computer programming
- specialized computer applications like music composition software, computer assisted drawing and drafting programs, mathematics modeling software, etc.

Listing computer skills is only a first step in assuring all our children become proficient information and technology users. A teacher supported scope and sequence of skills, well designed projects, and effective assessments are also critical. Many library media specialists will need to hone their own technology skills in order to remain effective information skills teachers. But such a curriculum holds tremendous opportunities for library media specialists to become vital, indispensable staff members, and for all children to master the skills they will need to thrive in an information rich future.

Computer Skills for Information Problem-Solving: A Curriculum Based on the Big Six Skills Approach ** copyright Michael B. Eisenberg, Doug Johnson & Robert E. Berkowitz

1. Task Definition:

The first step in the information problem-solving process is to recognize that an information need exists, to define the problem, and to identify the types and amount of information needed. In terms of technology, students will be able to:

A. Use e-mail, and online discussion groups (e.g., listservs, newsgroups) on the Internet to communicate with teachers regarding assignments, tasks, and information-problems.*

B. Use e-mail, and online discussion groups (e.g.,listservs, newsgroups) on the Internet to generate topics and problems and to facilitate cooperative activities among groups of students locally and globally.*

C. Use desktop conferencing, e-mail, and groupware software on local area networks to communicate with teachers regarding assignments, tasks, and information problems.

D. Use desktop conferencing, e-mail, and groupware software on local area networks to generate topics and problems and to facilitate cooperative activities among groups of students locally.

E. Use computer brainstorming or idea generating software to define or refine the information problem. This includes developing a research question or perspective on a topic.

2. Information Seeking Strategies:

Once the information problem has been formulated, the student must consider all possible information sources and develop a plan for searching. Students will be able to:

A. Assess the value of various types of electronic resources for data gathering, including databases, CD-ROM resources, commercial and Internet online resources, electronic reference works, community and government information electronic resources.*

B. Identify and apply specific criteria for evaluating computerized electronic resources.

C. Assess the value of e-mail, and online discussion groups (e.g., listservs, newsgroups) on the Internet as part of a search of the current literature or in relation to the information task.

D. Use a computer to generate modifiable flow charts, Gantt charts, time lines, organizational charts, project plans and calendars which will help the student plan and organize complex or group information problem-solving tasks.

3. Location and Access:

After students determine their priorities for information seeking, they must locate information from a variety of resources and access specific information found within individual resources. Students will be able to:

A. Locate and use appropriate computer resources and technologies available within the school library media center, including those on the library media center's local area network, (e.g., online catalogs, periodical indexes, full-text sources, multimedia computer stations, CD-ROM stations, online terminals, scanners, digital cameras).

B. Locate and use appropriate computer resources and technologies available throughout the school including those available through local area networks (e.g., full-text resources, CD-ROMs, productivity software, scanners, digital cameras).

C. Locate and use appropriate computer resources and technologies available beyond the school through the Internet (e.g., newsgroups, listservs, WWW sites via Netscape, Lynx or another browser, gopher, ftp sites, online public access library catalogs, commercial databases and online services, other community, academic, and government resources).*

D. Know the roles and computer expertise of the people working in the school library media center and elsewhere who might provide information or assistance.

E. Use electronic reference materials (e.g., electronic encyclopedias, dictionaries, biographical reference sources, atlases, geographic databanks, thesauri, almanacs, fact books) available through local area networks, stand-alone workstations, commercial online vendors, or the Internet.

F. Use the Internet or commercial computer networks to contact experts and help and referral services.*

G. Conduct self initiated electronic surveys conducted through e-mail, listservs or newsgroups.*

H. Use organizational systems and tools specific to electronic information sources that assist in finding specific and general information (e.g., indexes, tables of contents, user's instructions and manuals, legends, boldface and italics, graphic clues and icons, cross-references, Boolean logic strategies, time lines, hypertext links, knowledge trees, URLs etc.) including the use of:
   1. search tools and commands for stand-alone, CD-ROM, and online databases and services (e.g., DIALOG commands, America Online, UMI, Mead);
   2. search tools and commands for searching the Internet (e.g., Yahoo, Lycos, WebCrawler, Veronica, Archie).*

4. Use of Information:

After finding potentially useful resources, students must engage (read, view, listen) the information to determine its relevance and then extract the relevant information. Students will be able to:

A. Connect and operate the computer technology needed to access information, and read the guides and manuals associated with such tasks.

B. View, download, decompress and open documents and programs from Internet sites and archives.*
C. Cut and paste information from an electronic source into a personal document complete with proper citation.
D. Take notes and outline with a word processor or similar productivity program.
E. Record electronic sources of information and locations of those sources to properly cite and credit in footnotes, endnotes, and bibliographies.
F. Use electronic spreadsheets, databases, and statistical software to process and analyze statistical data.
G. Analyze and filter electronic information in relation to the task, rejecting non-relevant information.

5. Synthesis:

Students must organize and communicate the results of the information problem-solving effort. Students will be able to:

A. Classify and group information using a word processor, database or spreadsheet.
B. Use word processing and desktop publishing software to create printed documents, applying keyboard skills equivalent to at least twice the rate of handwriting speed.
C. Create and use computer-generated graphics and art in various print and electronic presentations.
D. Use electronic spreadsheet software to create original spreadsheets.
E. Generate charts, tables and graphs using electronic spreadsheets and other graphing programs.
F. Use database/file management software to create original databases.
G. Use presentation software (e.g. *PowerPoint, HyperStudio, Aldus Persuasion*) to create electronic slide shows and to generate overheads and slides.
H. Create hypermedia and multimedia productions with digital video and audio.
I. Create World Wide Web pages and sites using hypertext markup language (HTML).*
J. Use e-mail, ftp, and other telecommunications capabilities to share information, products, and files.*
K. Use specialized computer applications as appropriate for specific tasks, e.g., music composition software, computer assisted drawing and drafting programs, mathematics modeling software.
L. Properly cite and credit electronic sources of information in footnotes, endnotes, and bibliographies.

6. Evaluation:

Evaluation focuses on how well the final product meets the original task (effectiveness) and the process of how well students carried out the information problem-solving process (efficiency). Students may evaluate their own work and process or be evaluated by others (i.e. classmates, teachers, library media staff, parents). Students will be able to:

A. Evaluate electronic presentations in terms of both the content and format.
B. Use spell and grammar checking capabilities of word processing and other software to edit and revise their work.
C. Apply legal principles and ethical conduct related to information technology related to copyright and plagiarism.
D. Understand and abide by telecomputing etiquette when using e-mail, newsgroups, listservs and other Internet functions.*
E. Understand and abide by acceptable use policies in relation to use of the Internet and other electronic technologies.
F. Use e-mail, and online discussion groups (e.g., listservs, newsgroups) on local area networks and the Internet to communicate with teachers and others regarding their performance on assignments, tasks, and information-problems.*
G. Use desktop conferencing, e-mail, and groupware software on local area networks to communicate with teachers and others regarding student performance on assignments, tasks, and information problems.
H. Thoughtfully reflect on the use of electronic resources and tools throughout the process.

Addendum:

Included here are skills and knowledge related to technology that are not part of the computer and information

The Big Six Skills Approach to Information Problem Solving

copyright Eisenberg and Berkowitz, 1987.

The Big Six is an information literacy curriculum, an information problem-solving process, and a set of skills which provide a strategy for effectively and efficiently meeting information needs. The Big Six Skills approach can be used whenever students are in a situation, academic or personal, which requires information to solve a problem, make a decision or complete a task. This model is transferable to school, personal, and work applications, as well as all content areas and the full range of grade levels. When taught collaboratively with content area teachers in concert with content-area objectives, it serves to ensure that students are information literate.

The Big Six:

1. Task Definition
- 1.1 Define the task (the information problem)
- 1.2 Identify information needed in order to complete the task (to solve the information problem)

2. Information Seeking Strategies
- 2.1 Brainstorm all possible sources
- 2.2 Select the best sources

3. Location and Access
- 3.1 Locate sources
- 3.2 Find information within the source

4. Use of Information
- 4.1 Engage in the source (read, hear, view, touch)
- 4.2 Extract relevant information

5. Synthesis
- 5.1 Organize information from multiple sources
- 5.2 Present the information

6. Evaluation
- 6.1 Judge the process (efficiency)
- 6.2 Judge the product (effectiveness)

technology curriculum. These items should be learned in context, i.e., as students are working through various assignments and information problems using technology. Students will be able to:

A. Know and use basic computer terminology.
B. Operate various pieces of hardware and software--particularly operating systems--and be able to handle basic maintenance.
C. Understand the basics of computer programming. Specific courses in computer programming should be part of the school's curricular offerings.
D. Understand and articulate the relationship and impact of information technology on careers, society, culture, and their own lives.

Note: Permission is granted for educational use or reprint of all or parts of this curriculum as long as the authors are properly and prominently credited.
* Items are specific to Internet use.
**This curriculum guide is an excerpt from Computer Skills for Information Problem-Solving: Learning and Teaching Technology in Context, ERIC Digest (1996, March), prepared by Michael B. Eisenberg and Doug Johnson for the ERIC Clearinghouse on Information & Technology, Syracuse, NY. (ED number pending, IR 055 809)

References and Suggested Reading

American Association of School Librarians. (1995, November). Information literacy: A position paper on information problem solving. Emergency Librarian, 23(2), 20-23. (EJ number pending, IR 531 873). Also available from the American Association of School Librarians.
California Media and Library Educators Association Staff. (1993). *From library skills to information literacy: A handbook for the 21st century*. Englewood, CO: Libraries Unlimited, Inc. (ISBN: 0-931510-49-X)
Coulehan, J. L. (1995). Using electronic mail for a small-group curriculum in ethical and social issues. *Academic Medicine*, 70(2), 158-163. (EJ 499 651)
Doyle, C. S. (1994). *Information literacy in an information society: A concept for the information age*. Syracuse, NY: ERIC Clearinghouse on Information & Technology. (ED 372 763)
Eisenberg, M. & Berkowitz, B. (1988). *Curriculum initiative: An agenda and strategy for library media programs*. Norwood, NJ: Ablex.
Eisenberg, M. B. & Berkowitz, R. E. (1992). Information problem-solving: The big six skills approach. *School Library Media Activities Monthly*, 8(5), 27-29,37,42. (EJ 438 023)
Eisenberg, M. B. & Ely, D. P. (1993). Plugging into the "Net." *Emergency Librarian*, 21(2), 8-16. (EJ 471 260)
Eisenberg, M. B. & Small, R.V. (1993). Information-based education: An investigation of the nature and role of information attributes in education. *Information Processing and Management*, 29(2), 263-275. (EJ 462 841)
Eisenberg, M. B. & Spitzer, K. L. (1991). Information technology and services in schools. In M. E. Williams (Ed.), *Annual Review of Information Science and Technology: Vol. 26*. (pp. 243-285). Medford, NJ: Learned Information, Inc. (EJ 441 688)
Garland, K. (1995). The information search process: A study of elements associated with meaningful research tasks. *School Libraries Worldwide*, 1(1), 41-53. (EJ 503 407)
Johnson, D. (1995). Captured by the web: K-12 schools and the world-wide web. *MultiMedia Schools*, 2(2), 24-30. (EJ 499 841)
Johnson, D. (1995). The new and improved school library: How one district planned for the future. *School Library Journal*, 41(6), 36-39. (EJ 505 448)
Johnson, D. (1995). Student access to the Internet: Librarians and teachers working together to teach higher level survival skills. *Emergency Librarian*, 22(3), 8-12. (EJ 497 895)
Kuhlthau, C. C. (1993). Implementing a process approach to information skills: A study identifying indicators of success in library media programs. *School Library Media Quarterly*, 22(1), 11-18. (EJ 473 063)
Kuhlthau, C. C. (1995). The process of learning from information. *School Libraries Worldwide*, 1(1), 1-12. (EJ 503 404)
Mankato Schools Information Literacy Curriculum Guideline. Internet WWW page, at URL: http://www.isd77.k12.mn.us/resources/infolit.html (version current at 11 March 1996).
McNally, M. J. & Kulhthau, C. C. (1994). Information search process in science education. *Reference Librarian, 44*, 53-60. (EJ 488 273)
Minnesota Department of Education. (1989). *Model learner outcomes for educational media and technology*. St. Paul, MN: Author. (ED 336 070)
Moursund, D. (1995, December). Effective practices (part 2): Productivity tools. *Learning and Leading With Technology*, 23(4), 5-6.
Pappas, M. L. (1993, September). A vision of school library media centers in an electronic information age. *School Library Media Activities Monthly*, 10(1), 32-34,38. (EJ 469 122)
Pappas, M. L. (1995). Information skills for electronic resources. *School Library Media Activities Monthly*, 11(8), 39-40. (EJ 499 875)
Todd, R. J. (1995). Information literacy: Philosophy, principles, and practice. *School Libraries Worldwide*, 1(1), 54-68. (EJ 503 408)
Todd, R. J. (1995). Integrated information skills instruction: Does it make a difference? *School Library Media Quarterly*, 23(2), 133-138. (EJ 497 921)
Wisconsin Educational Media Association. (1993). *Information literacy: A position paper on information problem-solving*. Madison, WI: WEMA Publications. (ED 376 817). (Portions adapted from Michigan State Board of Education's Position Paper on Information Processing Skills, 1992).

This ERIC Digest was prepared by Michael B. Eisenberg, director of the ERIC Clearinghouse on Information & Technology and professor of Information Studies, Syracuse University, Syracuse, NY, and Doug Johnson, district media supervisor for Mankato Public Schools, Mankato MN.

ERIC Digests are in the public domain and may be freely reproduced and disseminated.

ERIC Clearinghouse on Information & Technology, Syracuse University, 4-194 Center for Science & Technology, Syracuse, New York 13244-4100; (315) 443-3640; (800) 464-9107; Fax: (315) 443-5448; Internet: eric@ericir.syr.edu

---

This publication was prepared with funding from the Office of Educational Research and Improvement, U.S. Department of Education, under contract no. RR93002009. The opinions expressed in this report do not necessarily reflect the positions of OERI or ED.

Information Services—Including Technology

Resources Provision	Online catalogs, information retrieval, electronic resources (including CD-ROM nets), WWW/net resources, AskERIC, KidsConnect, online discussion groups (listservs, newsgroups)
Direct Information Service	AskERIC, KidsConnect, e-mail, online discussion groups (listservs, newsgroups), LM_NET
Reading Guidance	Interactive CD-ROMs, collaborative projects on the Internet, e-mail, online discussion groups (listservs, newsgroups)
Curriculum Consultation/ Development	E-mail, online discussion groups (listservs, newsgroups), AskERIC, collaborative projects on the Internet, groupware, production and presentation software/ hardware

Think Sheet

Part IV:

Instructional Design (and Redesign)

Introduction

Learning the Big6 is cumulative—i.e., students gain proficiency in the process and skills over time. We also emphasize that the Big6 Skills are best learned in two contexts: the context of the overall process itself, and within the context of real needs—curricular or personal.

In order to ensure that students learn essential Big6 Skills in these two contexts means designing learning events that help students to learn the overall Big6 process as well as the individual Big6 Skills. This "systematic instructional design" takes place on two levels:

1. The micro level—designing integrated instructional units and lessons
2. The macro level—planning for integrated curriculum on the classroom, grade, subject area, or overall school level.

The activities, worksheets, and readings in Part IV focus on the micro level. Developing skills in analysis and planning on the macro level is covered in Part VII.

The goal in micro instructional design is to help classroom, library, and technology teachers learn to integrate Big6 units and lessons. The subject area content of such units and lessons are provided within school- or classroom-defined curriculum. As part of any classroom learning experience, students must engage in various Big6 information problem-solving stages. Students use the Big6 whenever a teacher requires them to do the following:

- Listen to a lecture or video
- Conduct an experiment
- Read from a textbook
- Complete a worksheet
- Make a project
- Take a test
- Select a topic
- Do some homework.

It is possible and highly desirable to weave Big6 instruction throughout existing or planned classroom instruction. THE BIG6 IS NOT AN ADD-ON! Instruction in the Big6 is integrated with classroom instruction and is integral to success in completing subject area goals and objectives.

The following activity sheet and worksheets focus attention on the curriculum-Big6 connection. One key requirement for educators is to recognize the Big6 Skills within units and lessons. To this end, the questions and forms help teachers (classroom, library, and technology) to decide upon (1) the important elements of instruction, (2) the key skills for student success—as well as where they may have difficulties, and (3) the specifics of delivering integrated instruction through units and lessons.

Part IV concludes with the ERIC Digest, "Motivation in Instructional Design," by Dr. Ruth Small. This Digest explains the ARCS Model of Motivational Design. ARCS stands for:

- Attention
- Relevance
- Confidence
- Satisfaction.

We find that designing integrated units and lessons from an ARCS model guarantees effective Big6 and content area learning.

Activity Sheet

This exercise will help you analyze the Collaborative Instructional Unit Planning Process.

Developing Big6™ Understandings: Worksheet 4-1

Curriculum Context: Create a typical, integrated curriculum situation. Describe one or two activities that relate to each of the Big6 Skills.

Big6 Skills	Activities
1. Task Definition 1.1 Define the problem. 1.2 Identify the information needed.	
2. Information Seeking Strategies 2.1 Determine all possible sources. 2.2 Select the best source.	
3. Location & Access 3.1 Locate sources. 3.2 Find information within sources.	
4. Use of Information 4.1 Engage (e.g., read, hear, view). 4.2 Extract relevant information.	
5. Synthesis 5.1 Organize information from multiple sources. 5.2 Present the result.	
6. Evaluation 6.1 Judge the result (effectiveness). 6.2 Judge the process (efficiency).	

Unit & Lesson Implementation

Big6™ Unit Planning Guide

© Eisenberg/Berkowitz, 1995

Teacher: **Subject:**

Unit/Topic:

Collaborative Instructional Unit Planning: Key Questions to Ask and Answer
1. What do we want students to understand?
2. What are the content area objectives?
3. What are the Big6 Skills objectives?
4. Where does this fit into the overall curriculum?
5. What will students do to demonstrate their new knowledge or skill?
6. How will the instructional unit be managed? (grouping, time frame, materials, etc.)

Unit & Lesson Implementation

Big6 Unit Planning Guide

© Eisenberg/Berkowitz, 1987

Teacher:	**Subject:**
Unit/Topic:	

Big6 Skills	**Collaborative Instructional Planning Guide: Activities**	**Level of Instruction**	**LMS and/or Teacher**	**Focus**
1. Task Definition 1.1 Define the problem. 1.2 Identify the information needed.				
2. Information Seeking Strategies 2.1 Determine all possible sources. 2.2 Select the best source.				
3. Location & Access 3.1 Locate sources. 3.2 Find information within sources.				
4. Use of Information 4.1 Engage (e.g., read, hear, view). 4.2 Extract relevant information.				
5. Synthesis 5.1 Organize information from multiple sources. 5.2 Present the result.				
6. Evaluation 6.1 Judge the result (effectiveness). 6.2 Judge the process (efficiency).				

Unit & Lesson Implementation

Instructional Unit Design Format

Unit:
Audience:

Overview:
Rationale:
Subject Area Objectives:
Big6 Objectives:
Activities:
Evaluation:
Materials:
Follow-up/Supplemental Activities:

Unit & Lesson Implementation

Lesson Plan Format

Subject:

Teacher:

Lesson Name:

Location:

Class:

Unit Context:

Date:

Activities	Big6 Skills	Subject Area Objectives

Materials/Resources:

Evaluation:

Notes:

July 1997 EDO-IR-97-06

Motivation in Instructional Design

by Ruth V. Small

Introduction

Developing life-long learners who are intrinsically motivated, display intellectual curiosity, find learning enjoyable, and continue seeking knowledge after their formal instruction has ended has always been a major goal of education. Early motivational research was conducted primarily in the workplace, and centered on ways to motivate industrial workers to work harder, faster, and better.

More recent motivational research focuses on the identification of effective techniques for enhancing instructional design, improving classroom management, and meeting the needs of diverse student populations (Wlodkowski, 1981). Learning-motivation researchers are applying some of the same theories and concepts found to be effective in industry to the development of motivational models that enhance the teaching-learning environment. One such model is the ARCS Model of Motivational Design developed by John M. Keller of Florida State University (Keller, 1983,1987). ARCS is a systematic model for designing motivating instruction. This digest will describe the ARCS Model, and will outline some of the ways in which ARCS components may be applied to instructional design.

The ARCS Model of Motivational Design

The ARCS Model of Motivational Design is a well-known and widely applied model of instructional design. Simple, yet powerful, the ARCS Model is rooted in a number of motivational theories and concepts, (see Keller, 1983) most notably expectancy-value theory (e.g. Vroom, 1964; Porter and Lawler, 1968).

In expectancy-value theory, "effort" is identified as the major measurable motivational outcome. For "effort" to occur, two necessary prerequisites are specified — (1) the person must value the task and (2) the person must believe he or she can succeed at the task. Therefore, in an instructional situation, the learning task needs to be presented in a way that is engaging and meaningful to the student, and in a way that promotes positive expectations for the successful achievement of learning objectives.

The ARCS Model identifies four essential strategy components for motivating instruction:

- **[A]**ttention strategies for arousing and sustaining curiosity and interest;
- **[R]**elevance strategies that link to learners' needs, interests, and motives;
- **[C]**onfidence strategies that help students develop a positive expectation for successful achievement; and
- **[S]**atisfaction strategies that provide extrinsic and intrinsic reinforcement for effort (Keller, 1983).

Keller (1987) breaks each of the four ARCS components down into three strategy sub-components. The strategy sub-components and instructionally relevant examples are shown below.

✎ Attention

- ***Perceptual Arousal:*** provide novelty, surprise, incongruity or uncertainty. Ex. The teacher places a sealed box covered with question marks on a table in front of the class.
- ***Inquiry Arousal:*** stimulate curiosity by posing questions or problems to solve. Ex. The teacher presents a scenario of a problem situation and asks the class to brainstorm possible solutions based on what they have learned in the lesson.
- ***Variability:*** incorporate a range of methods and media to meet students' varying needs. Ex. After displaying and reviewing each step in the process on the overhead projector, the teacher divides the class into teams and assigns each team a set of practice problems.

✎ Relevance

- ***Goal Orientation:*** present the objectives and useful purpose of the instruction and specific methods for successful achievement.
  Ex. The teacher explains the objectives of the lesson.
- ***Motive Matching:*** match objectives to student needs and motives. Ex. The teacher allows the students to present their projects in writing or orally to accommodate different learning needs and styles.
- ***Familiarity:*** present content in ways that are understandable and that are related to the learners' experience and values. Ex. The teacher asks the students to provide examples from their own experiences for the concept presented in class.

✎ Confidence

- ***Learning Requirements:*** inform students about learning and performance requirements and assessment criteria. Ex. The teacher provides students with a list of assessment criteria for their research projects and circulates examples of exemplary projects from past years.
- ***Success Opportunities:*** provide challenging and meaningful opportunities for successful learning. Ex. The teacher allows the students to practice extracting and summarizing information from various sources and then provides feedback before the students begin their research projects.
- ***Personal Responsibility:*** link learning success to students'

personal effort and ability. Ex. The teacher provides written feedback on the quality of the students' performance and acknowledges the students' dedication and hard work.

✎ Satisfaction

- ***Intrinsic Reinforcement:*** encourage and support intrinsic enjoyment of the learning experience. Ex. The teacher invites former students to provide testimonials on how learning these skills helped them with subsequent homework and class projects.
- ***Extrinsic Rewards:*** provide positive reinforcement and motivational feedback. Ex. The teacher awards certificates to students as they master the complete set of skills.
- ***Equity:*** maintain consistent standards and consequences for success. Ex. After the term project has been completed, the teacher provides evaluative feedback using the criteria described in class.

Motivation Assessment Instruments

Since the ARCS Model was introduced in the early 1980's, several instruments have been developed for assessing the motivational quality of instructional situations. The Instructional Materials Motivation Survey (IMMS) (Keller, 1987) asks students to rate 36 ARCS-related statements in relation to the *instructional materials* they have just used. Some examples are:

- "These materials are eye-catching." (Attention)
- "It is clear to me how the content of this material is related to things I already know." (Relevance)
- "As I worked on this lesson, I was confident that I could learn the content." (Confidence)
- "Completing the exercises in this lesson gave me a satisfying feeling of accomplishment." (Satisfaction)

Keller and Keller (1989) developed the Motivational Delivery Checklist, a 47-item ARCS-based instrument for evaluating the motivational characteristics of an instructor's *classroom delivery*. Examples of items related to each ARCS component are:

- "Uses questions to pose problems or paradoxes." (Attention)
- "Uses language and terminology appropriate to learners and their context." (Relevance)
- "Provides feedback on performance promptly." (Confidence)
- "Makes statements giving recognition and credit to learners as appropriate." (Satisfaction)

The Website Motivational Analysis Checklist (WebMAC) (Small,1997) is an instrument used for designing and assessing the motivational quality of World Wide Web sites. WebMAC builds on Keller's work (1987a; 1987b; 1989), Taylor's Value-Added Model (1986), and the research on relevance and information retrieval (e.g. Schamber, 1994). Still in development and testing, WebMAC identifies 60 items that are categorized according to four general characteristics: Engaging, Meaningful, Organized, and Enjoyable. Some examples of items are:

- "Eye-catching title and/or visual on home page." (Engaging)
- "User-controlled type of information accessed." (Meaningful)
- "Logical sequence of information." (Organized)
- "Links to other websites of interest." (Enjoyable)

Summary

The ARCS Model of Motivational Design is an easy-to-apply, heuristic approach to increasing the motivational appeal of instruction. ARCS provides a useful framework for both the design and improvement of the motivational quality of a range of informational entities—from classroom instruction to Internet resources—and increases the likelihood that these entities will be used and enjoyed.◆

References and Related Readings

Chemotti, J.T. (1992, June). From nuclear arms to Hershey's kisses: Strategies for motivating students. *School Library Media Activities Monthly, 8*(10), 34-36. (EJ 446 223)

Keller, J.M.(1983). *Motivational design of instruction. In C.M. Reigeluth (Ed.). Instructional design theories and models: An overview of their current status.* Hillsdale, NJ: Erlbaum.

Keller, J.M. (1987a, Oct.). Strategies for stimulating the motivation to learn. *Performance and Instruction, 26*(8), 1-7. (EJ 362 632)

Keller, J.M. (1987b). *IMMS: Instructional materials motivation survey.* Florida State University.

Keller, J.M. & Keller, B.H. (1989). *Motivational delivery checklist.* Florida State University.

Porter, L.W. & Lawler, E.E. (1968). *Managerial attitudes and performance.* Homewood, IL: Dorsey Press.

Schamber, L. (1994). Relevance and information behavior. *Annual Review of Information Science and Technolgy*, Medford, NJ: Learned Information, Inc. (EJ 491 620)

Small, R.V. (1992, Apr.). Taking AIM: Approaches to instructional motivation. *School Library Media Activities Monthly, 8*(8), 32-34.

Small, R.V. (1997). *Assessing the motivational quality of world wide websites.* ERIC Clearinghouse on Information and Technology. (ED number pending, IR 018 331)

Taylor, R.S. (1986). *Value-added processes in information systems.* Norwood, NJ: Ablex. (ISBN: 0-89391-273-5)

Vroom, V.H. (1964). *Work and motivation.* New York: Wiley.

Wlodkowski, R.J. (1981). Making sense our of motivation: A systematic model to consolidate motivational constructs across theories. *Educational Psychologist, 16*(2), 101-110.

This ERIC Digest was prepared by Ruth V. Small, associate professor of Information Studies at Syracuse University, Syracuse, New York.

ERIC Digests are in the public domain and may be freely reproduced and disseminated.

ERIC Clearinghouse on Information & Technology, Syracuse University, 4-194 Center for Science and Technology, Syracuse, New York 13244-4100; (315) 443-3640; (800) 464-9107; Fax: (315) 443-5448; E-mail: eric@ericir.syr.edu; URL: http://ericir.syr.edu/ithome

This publication was prepared with funding from the Office of Educational Research and Improvement, U.S. Department of Education under contract no. RR93002009. The opinions expressed in this report do not necessarily reflect the positions of OERI or ED.

Think Sheet

Part V:

Assessment

Introduction

✓ *Have students learned what was intended?*

✓ *Are students proficient in the overall Big6 process?*

✓ *Are students able to solve information problems across a range of situations, subjects, and settings?*

✓ *Are students skilled in each of the Big6 stages and sub-stages?*

Answering these questions is what assessment is all about. Assessment is often dreaded because it comes across as negative and difficult to accomplish. This need not be the case. Assessment can be used to recognize strengths and highlight skills that need improving, and assessment can be handled in a straight-forward manner. We emphasize that teachers should communicate expectations as well as the techniques that will be used to evaluate students' performance in relation to expectations. The evidence required to assess Big6 proficiency can be gathered within the context of existing assignments, tests, products, and others forms of assessment.

Assessment from a Big6 perspective means going beyond simply whether the students learned the content that was taught. Teachers must also determine students' abilities in terms of the processes involved. For example, it is important to know whether students were able to clearly articulate their assignment and the information needed (Task Definition) or whether they were able to acquire the information they were supposed to get (Information Seeking Strategies and Location & Access). And, could they pull out the valuable information and apply it to the task (Use of Information and Synthesis)? Lastly, were the students themselves able to recognize and correct deficiencies in their work (Evaluation)? In other words, classroom teachers and teacher-librarians must be able to assess performance within the information problem-solving process itself and then develop ways for students to address deficiencies and problems.

We also believe that assessment is the responsibility of students as well as teachers. Students must be able to assess the results of their efforts by analyzing the effectiveness of their product and their efficient use of the information problem-solving strategy. It is crucial to help students learn to:

- Value and recognize quality work
- Reflect on the ways they go about tackling assignments and tasks
- Determine how they can improve
- Recognize the relationship between self-discipline and achievement
- Gain self-confidence in solving information problems.

Students frequently have no idea why they scored as they did on an assignment. At best, they might speculate on what they did wrong. It's more likely that they won't even think about it. Students must be encouraged to assume ownership of their own work—through self-assessment. Students can and must also learn this process of assessment. They need to know how to identify the factors that define a job well done, determine whether they found all of them, and compare their product with an exemplar.

But that is not enough. Students must then gauge whether they were properly engaged in the process. They should be able to determine whether they were efficient in terms of time management, product development, or even assessment. Additionally, students must develop skills in judging their effectiveness. They need to know that they can recognize an exemplar when presented with one.

It's important to take the guesswork out of assessment. If a student judges her work to be "good or excellent," but the teacher rates it as just "fair or adequate," there's a gap between teacher and student understanding—and that's a clear problem. In learning and using the Big6, we hope that students and teachers can eliminate that gap. This can happen by helping students learn to assess their own products and skills according to the same criteria that teachers use. We talk about having students think like their teachers or "getting inside their teachers' heads." Students can learn to assume ownership for their own learning, to diagnose problems, and to select solutions.

The exercise in Part V of the *Workshop Handbook* is designed to help educators develop competence in assessing students' Big6 abilities. The aids—particularly the Big6 Scoring Guides—are useful mechanisms for documenting and planning assessment criteria and evidence.

For example, Bob's in-service workshop on assessment is built around the "Postcard" Assessment Exercise. Bob asks the teachers to analyze the assignment from a Big6 perspective. What is required of the students? What are the key Big6 Skills? What criteria will be used to assess student performance? Bob and the teachers (sometimes working in groups) then start to fill in the Big6 Scoring Guide matrix:

1. First, members need to agree upon a grading scale (e.g., "Highly Competent to Not Yet Acceptable).

2. Next, members discuss which stages of the Big6 are represented or emphasized in the assignment in some way. They determine the "degree of focus" for each Big6 Skill to be assessed and assign a relative percentage in the rightmost column.

3. Then teachers define the criteria within each Big6 Skill and level, for example, whatever the "best case" would be for Task Definition becomes the expectation for Highly Competent. Bob and the teachers work through each level down to "Not Yet Acceptable."

4. The matrix is completed by determining what evidence will be used to assess student performance. They go through each of the Big6 trying to determine the qualities and quantities of work expected and the evidence required to measure the work. Last, the weight or percent of focus is finalized.

After the Scoring Guide is defined, the teachers break into groups to assess the postcards. They gain experience applying their assessment tool to actual student work. Debriefing includes discussing the value and approaches to assessing both the Big6 process and the final products of student work.

The article on Big6 Scoring Guides is from *The Big6 Newsletter*. It provides further explanation about the various forms and how to use them.

Assessment Exercise
Assessment Activity

Assessment Exercise

Review the following instructional activity. Determine the Big6 Skills attributes, focus, and the criteria to assess student performance.

You have just won the grand prize in the Spanish 2 Cultural Sweepstakes. The prize is an all expenses paid trip to South America, Central America, and Spain. Because Mrs. Hoffman is such a terrific teacher, you have decided to write her two postcards to describe your trip.

Your task is to write two picture postcards, either from a Spanish speaking country in South America, Central America, or from Spain. One card's content should focus on topics from the "social" list below and the second card should focus on topics from the "political" list below.

The front of each postcard must have a graphic (picture or drawing) which illustrates the content of the written message.

Social:

_____ recreation

_____ clothing

_____ celebrations

_____ customs and traditions

_____ sports/games

_____ food

_____ communication

_____ religion

_____ family life

_____ school

_____ art

_____ shopping

_____ housing

_____ music

_____ entertainment

Political:

_____ government structure

_____ history

_____ currency

_____ employment

_____ climate

_____ regions (beaches, mountains, etc.)

_____ historical personalities

_____ population statistics

_____ exports/imports

_____ sites of interests/places to visit

_____ current events

_____ historical landmarks

Assessment Exercise

Assessment Exercise

Dear Mrs. Hoffman,

Madrid is great! Shopping here is excellent. The malls here are gigantic and beautiful (See front) Most malls have more than 150 stores. Madrid is called the "capitol of joy and contentment." Our tour guide told us that the UN had to invent the word 'la movida' to describe Madrid's bustling nightlife! Madrid's restaurants offer a variety of food from around the world. The city's most popular dish is Madrid Stew. Some of ingredients are potatoes, chickpeas, black pudding and meat. There are more than 140 art galleries in Madrid. Every year, there is a Contemporary Art Fair. It is one of the most important art fairs in the world. Well, I have to go. We're going to an open-air cafe for lunch. See you soon!

Katie

Mrs Hoffman
6200 Ontario Ctr. R
Ontario, NY
14520

Dear Mrs Hoffman,

Hi! I'm in Madrid. Yesterday, I visited the Plaza Mayor. It is the sight for many things such as: bullfights, dances, concerts, and fairs. Every Sunday, there is a stamp and coin show. There is a place in Madrid called 'zero kilometre'. It has been there ever since the 19th century. It is the distance marker for all the roads leading out of the city. My tour guide told me that the population of Madrid is about 3,124,000. That's almost three times the population of Barcelona! I was also told about Spain's exports. They are citrus fruits, olive oil, wine, footwear, and vegetables. I have to go now. We're going to the park for a picnic. See you later!

Katie

Mrs. Hoffman
6300 Ontario Ctr. Rc
Ontario, NY
14520

Assessment Exercise

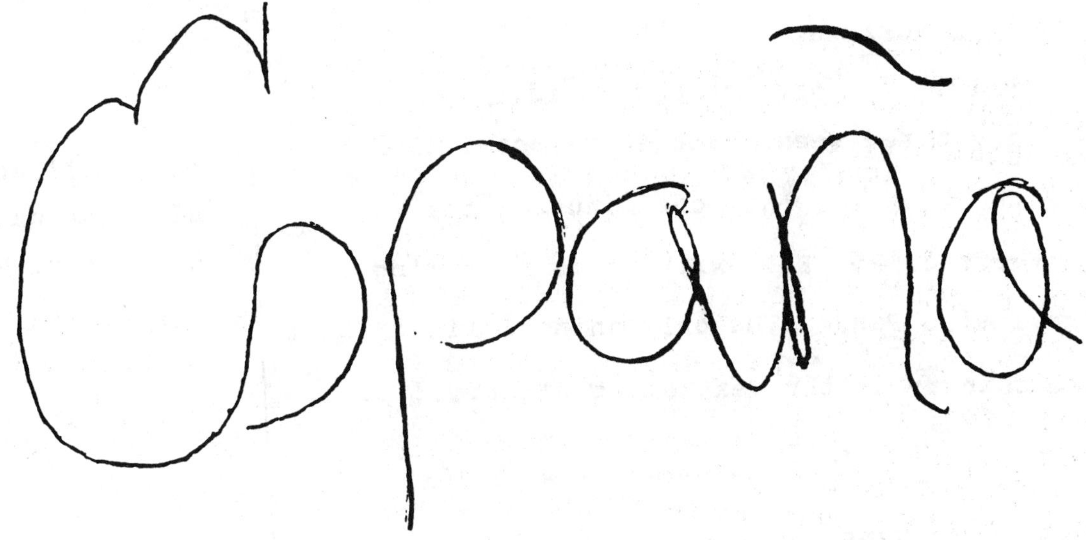

Assessment Exercise

Dear Mrs. Hoffman,

Brazil is very hot and humid.I was very tired when I got in my hotel room.And that was only one minute after I got out of my "El Taxi!" It is so boring here.I miss Panama!The only thing I liked about this country is the weather at night..........

Hasta Luego,

Sarah

Mrs. Hoffman
6200 ont.centr.Rd
ont. centr. N.Y
14568.

Dear Mrs. Hoffman,

Ohhh man... I just love those malls.They are humongous.They have 76 stores.One of them is all souveniers and party gifts,another is a history store with ancient jewels and other old stuff.Of course I'm talking about Brazil.I started to like it when I got used to the weather.Now I love this place............

C-Ya Later,

SARAH

Mrs. Hoffman
6200 ont. centr. rd.
Ont. Centr. N.Y. 14568

Assessment: Big6 Scoring Guides for Diagnosis and Prescription

Articles on assessment in the previous two issues focused on student self-assessment and introduced various techniques for conducting assessment. With all that's going on in schools, it's unrealistic to expect teachers, librarians, and even students to be able to add elaborate information skills assessment activities to what they already do. We need an effective and easy-to-use tool to help with assessment. Here it is: the Big6 Scoring Guide.

Big Six Scoring Guides are designed to communicate expectations for students' work and achievement in ways that students can understand and use. Big6 Scoring Guides focus on the process of solving information problems as well as the final result. Therefore, guides are useful both during and after working on assignments—for both formative and summative assessment.

Formative assessment, as explained in previous articles, involves diagnosing students' performance during learning so that adjustments can be made before students turn in their work. Adjustments may include:

- redirecting planned instruction to focus on areas where students are having trouble
- providing special learning activities not previously planned
- helping students to apply relevant technology tools
- redefining the problem or returning to a previous Big6 stage
- offering one-on-one tutoring
- brainstorming alternative approaches.

These types of adjustments are prescriptions for improving learning. Of course, Big6 Scoring Guides can also be used to assess final products: summative assessment. In working with teachers, we find that post-assignment debriefings—built around Big6 Scoring Guides—are effective ways of involving students in the assessment process.

To create Big6 Scoring Guides

1. Define the curriculum objectives within a Big6 context.
2. Determine which Big6 Skills are important (the focus) for this particular assignment.
3. Develop criteria across a scale (from "highly competent" to "not yet acceptable"). There may be more than one aspect to each criteria. Consider which aspects are essential.

Figure A: Muscular Action Worksheet

Your task is to design a controlled experiment to test the hypothesis below. Your experiment should be designed so that it can be conducted in a 15 to 20 minute period.

Hypothesis:

When there is an increase in muscular activity, there is a corresponding increase in the energy used by muscles. This energy increase causes heat as well as a corresponding increase in oxygen consumption.

Material:

Procedure:

Result: (tabulate data and represent in an appropriate graph)

Conclusion:

Questions:

- What variable(s) did you test?
- What are the constants?
- What was the experimental control?
- Evaluation/Scoring Guide

By Bob Berkowitz

4. Determine what evidence will be examined to determine student performance for each Big6 skill.

5. Conduct the assessment.

6. Share the assessment with students.

7. Revise as necessary.

For example, assume that completing Figure A is the task for students in ninth-grade biology studying "muscular activity." Figure B is the Big6 Scoring Guide designed to assess students' performance. This guide is designed to include multiple assessments—by student (S), teacher (T), and library media specialist (L). This allows students and teachers to quickly identify gaps in their views of perceived performance. Focusing on gaps can lead to clarification of misunderstandings and highlighting the need for further instruction.

The column labeled "Evidence" indicates the products or techniques used to assess specific skills. Examples of evidence include written, visual, or oral products, assignments, homework, projects, tests, observation, or even self-reflection. This is an essential piece of the Scoring Guide since it identifies the specific context for assessing student performance.

The last column, "Focus," relates to the relative importance of each skill being evaluated. It is not necessary or desirable to assess all Big6 skills equally in every learning situation. The assigned focus should be based on the goals and objectives of the unit in terms of Big6 skill development and content learning. For example, in the muscle example, a percentage of emphasis is assigned to each of the Big6 skills. Location & Access is not a skill emphasized in this situation while Task Definition, Information Seeking Strategy and Synthesis are.

continued on page 87

Figure B: Big6 Scoring Guide for Muscular Action

Big6™ Assessment Scoring Guide
Muscular Exercise

	Criteria									
Big6™ Skills Eisenberg/Berkowitz, ©1988		**Highly Competent** **10 points**		**Competent** **8 points**		**Adequate** **7 points**		**Not Yet Acceptable** **5 points**	**Evidence**	**Focus**
1. Task Definition 1.1 Define the problem. 1.2 Identify the information needed.	S T L	Experiment meets 15-20 minute requirement. Procedure tested: oxygen consumption and levels of heat.	S T L	Experiment limited to 15-20 minutes. Procedure tested: oxygen consumption or level of heat, but not both.	S T L	Experiment did not meet time requirement. Procedure tested: oxygen consumption or levels of heat, but not both.	S T L	Experiment did not meet time requirement. Procedure did not test for either: oxygen consumption or levels of heat.	Experiment	20%
2. Information Seeking Strategies 2.1 Determine all possible sources. 2.2 Select the best sources.	S T L	Procedure can be repeated exactly and produce the same results. Procedure tests the hypothesis.	S T L	Procedure tested the hypothesis, but is not easily followed.	S T L	Procedure tests the hypothesis, but is not easily followed, and does not give the same results.	S T L	Procedure does not test the hypothesis. Procedure cannot be repeated at all.	Procedure	40%
3. Location & Access 3.1 Locate sources. 3.2 Find information within sources.	S T L		S T L		S T L		S T L			
4. Use of Information 4.1 Engage (e.g., read hear, view, touch). 4.2 Extract relevant information.	S T L	Complete and accurate data tables. Complete and appropriate graphs.	S T L	Accurate data tables. Appropriate but incomplete graphs.	S T L	Incomplete data tables. Incomplete and inaccurate graphs.	S T L	No data tables. No graphs.	Results	10%
5. Synthesis 5.1 Organize information from multiple sources. 5.2 Present the result.	S T L	Appropriate conclusion. Answers all questions completely.	S T L	Appropriate conclusion. Answers all questions poorly.	S T L	Conclusion attempted, but inappropriate. Questions poorly answered and/or only some questions answered.	S T L	No conclusion. No questions answered.	Conclusion Question	20%
6. Evaluation 6.1 Judge the result. 6.2 Judge the process.	S T L	Scoring Guide thoughtfully completed.	S T L		S T L		S T L	Scoring Guide not completed.	Scoring Guide	10%

Eisenberg/Berkowitz, 1987

Assessment: Big6 Scoring Guides for Diagnosis and Prescription

continued from page 86

Figure C is an elementary curriculum example that uses a Big6 Scoring Guide in context. The curriculum context is a science lab experiment on the effects of light on seed growth. The Scoring Guide is an easy way to compare student and teacher assessment on key Big6 Skills: Location & Access, Use of Information, and Synthesis.

The hardest part of creating Big6 Scoring Guides is writing the specific statements of performance under each criteria and Big6 skill. We find that people get much better at this over time. Figure D is provided as a template to help you practice.

We also find that collaboration helps. Try working with library media specialists, other teachers, and even students. In fact, having students participate in creating their own Big6 Scoring Guides is an excellent technique for teaching the Big6 Skills of Task Definition and Evaluation.

Figure C: Elementary Science Experiment: Light and Seed Growth

Objectives:

1. To study the impact of light on seed growth.
2. To gather necessary materials and conduct an experiment.
3. To keep a daily journal of observations.
4. To write up a lab and draw logical conclusions.

Procedures:

Working in pairs, students are to:

1. Line two glasses with paper towels and stuff the inside of the glasses with more paper towels to hold the paper towel liner against the glass.
2. Place four bean seeds, evenly spaced and half-way down, between the glass and the paper towels.
3. Dampen the paper towels with water.
4. Put one glass in a dark cupboard or cabinet and place the other glass on a window sill.
5. Each day, moisten the paper towels in each glass.
6. Make observations in a journal each day for seven days. Note date, time, actions taken, observations.
7. Write up the experiment in scientific lab format. Include a written summary of results and a conclusion based on observations.

Assessment: Big6 Scoring Guide for Light and Seed Growth Experiment

Big6™ Skills	Expert Scientist	Scientist	Lab Assistant	Student
3 Location & Access 3.1 Locate sources. 3.2 Find information within sources.	Gathers lab materials: independently; appropriately.	Gathers lab materials: with some assistance; appropriately.	Needs assistance: missing some materials.	Needs assistance: missing most materials.
4. Use of Information 4.1 Engage (e.g., read hear, view, touch). 4.2 Extract relevant information.	Journal includes: daily entries; appropriate to task; accurate.	Journal includes: almost daily entries; appropriate to task; accurate.	Journal includes: some entries; inappropriate to task; accurate or inaccurate.	Journal includes: few or no entries.
5. Synthesis 5.1 Organize information from multiple sources. 5.2 Present the result.	Lab write-up complete and has proper format. Logical conclusion based on results.	Lab write-up not complete or problems with format. Logical conclusion based on results.	Lab write-up okay. Conclusion needs work.	Problems with lab write-up and/or format. Conclusion needs work.

Eisenberg/Berkowitz, 1987

Assessment: Big6 Scoring Guides for Diagnosis and Prescription
Figure D: Blank Big6 Scoring Guide

Big6™ Assessment Scoring Guide

Big6™ Skills Eisenberg/Berkowitz, ©1988	Criteria: Highly Competent 10 points	Competent 8 points	Adequate 7 points	Not Yet Acceptable 5 points	Evidence	Focus
1. Task Definition 1.1 Define the problem. 1.2 Identify the information needed.	S T L	S T L	S T L	S T L		
2. Information Seeking Strategies 2.1 Determine all possible sources. 2.2 Select the best sources.	S T L	S T L	S T L	S T L		
3. Location & Access 3.1 Locate sources. 3.2 Find information within sources.	S T L	S T L	S T L	S T L		
4. Use of Information 4.1 Engage (e.g., read hear, view, touch). 4.2 Extract relevant information.	S T L	S T L	S T L	S T L		
5. Synthesis 5.1 Organize information from multiple sources. 5.2 Present the result.	S T L	S T L	S T L	S T L		
6. Evaluation 6.1 Judge the result. 6.2 Judge the process.	S T L	S T L	S T L	S T L		

(S) Student, (T) Teacher, (L) Library Media Specialist

Eisenberg/Berkowitz, 1987

Reproduced from the *Big6 Newsletter*, January/February 1998, volume 1, number 3. For more information contact Linworth Publishing, Inc., 480 East Wilson Bridge Road, Suite L, Worthington, Ohio 43085-2372.

Assessment: Big6 Scoring Guides for Diagnosis and Prescription
Figure D: Blank Big6 Scoring Guide

Big6™ Assessment Scoring Guide

Big6™ Skills Eisenberg/Berkowitz, ©1988	Criteria Highly Competent 10 points	Competent 8 points	Adequate 7 points	Not Yet Acceptable 5 points	Evidence	Focus
1. Task Definition 1.1 Define the problem. 1.2 Identify the information needed.	S T L	S T L	S T L	S T L		
2. Information Seeking Strategies 2.1 Determine all possible sources. 2.2 Select the best sources.	S T L	S T L	S T L	S T L		
3. Location & Access 3.1 Locate sources. 3.2 Find information within sources.	S T L	S T L	S T L	S T L		
4. Use of Information 4.1 Engage (e.g., read hear, view, touch). 4.2 Extract relevant information.	S T L	S T L	S T L	S T L		
5. Synthesis 5.1 Organize information from multiple sources. 5.2 Present the result.	S T L	S T L	S T L	S T L		
6. Evaluation 6.1 Judge the result. 6.2 Judge the process.	S T L	S T L	S T L	S T L		

(S) Student, (T) Teacher, (L) Library Media Specialist

Eisenberg/Berkowitz, 1987

Reproduced from the *Big6 Newsletter*, January/February 1998, volume 1, number 3. For more information contact Linworth Publishing, Inc., 480 East Wilson Bridge Road, Suite L, Worthington, Ohio 43085-2372.

Think Sheet

Part VI:

Partnerships and Collaboration

Introduction

In our society today—in business, public service, and education—no one works or succeeds in isolation. This is particularly true of Big6 Skills instruction. Throughout this *Handbook*, in our other works, and in our workshops and presentations, we emphasize that effective Big6 Skills instruction is accomplished within the context of subject area, classroom learning.

We champion, promote, and work hard to facilitate an integrated, curriculum-based approach to skills development, and that requires true collaboration and partnership among classroom teachers, teacher-librarians, technology teachers, administrators, parents, community members, and students.

An integrated, collaborative approach is a departure from the traditional way that library, technology, and classroom teaching staff interact. In the past, school librarians would instruct students on library skills such as how to use dictionaries and encyclopedias or magazine indexes. This instruction was often done in isolation—far removed from the day-to-day activities of the classroom. More recently, we found computer teachers in computer labs teaching keyboarding, word processing, or information searching skills. Here too, the instruction was in isolation—without any connection to the subject content of classes.

Fortunately, these situations are changing. Teacher-librarians and computer teachers recognize that students learn better when instruction is linked to the needs of the classroom. We are seeing more and more partnerships among educators to design and implement learning situations in which skills and content are coordinated and integrated.

The material in this Part of the Big6 Workshop Handbook will assist you to understand the importance of collaboration and consider alternative approaches to forming partnerships within your schools and districts. The activity sheet and worksheets are designed to help make the Big6—classroom connections. Bob's article from *School Library Media Activities Monthly* addresses collaboration head-on, and Mike's article from *MultiMedia Schools* is a call-to-action to form meaningful information and technology teams in schools.

Overview

Information & Technology Skills for Student Success: The Big6™ Skills Approach

Implementation

- Context: the information problem-solving process (the Big6)
- Context: real needs in real situations
  - school, life, work
  - assignments: papers, reports, projects
- Approach:

  coordination ---> cooperation ---> collaboration

  - teachers, administrators, library media specialists, parents, community members

Partnership: School and Community Wide

- Classroom teachers
- Library and information specialists
- Technology teachers
- Administration and curriculum coordinators
- Parents!!!

Information Base

Compare and contrast the knowledge, attitudes, and skills of teachers, school library media specialists, and technology specialists.

	Teachers	Library Media Specialists	Technology Specialists
Knowledge			
Attitudes			
Skills			

Activity Sheet

This exercise will help you analyze the Collaborative Instructional Unit Planning Process.

Developing Big6™ Understandings: Worksheet 6-1

Curriculum Context: Create a typical, integrated curriculum situation. Describe one or two activities that relate to each of the Big6 Skills.

Big6 Skills	Activities
1. Task Definition 1.1 Define the problem. 1.2 Identify the information needed.	
2. Information Seeking Strategies 2.1 Determine all possible sources. 2.2 Select the best source.	
3. Location & Access 3.1 Locate sources. 3.2 Find information within sources.	
4. Use of Information 4.1 Engage (e.g., read, hear, view). 4.2 Extract relevant information.	
5. Synthesis 5.1 Organize information from multiple sources. 5.2 Present the result.	
6. Evaluation 6.1 Judge the result (effectiveness). 6.2 Judge the process (efficiency).	

Developing Big6™ Understandings: Worksheet 6-2

Instructional Strategies Development Sheet

List and describe alternative generic instructional strategies for each of the Big6 Skills.

1. Task Definition

1.1 Define the task (the information problem).
1.2 Identify information needed in order to complete the task (to solve the information problem).

2. Information Seeking Strategies

2.1 Determine the range of possible sources.
2.2 Evaluate the possible sources to determine priorities.

Developing Big6^{TM} Understandings: Worksheet 6-2

Instructional Strategies Development Sheet (continued)

3. Location & Access

3.1 Locate sources (intellectually and physically).
3.2 Find information within sources.

4. Use of Information

4.1 Engage (e.g., read, hear, view) the information in a source.
4.2 Extract information from a source.

Developing Big6™ Understandings: Worksheet 6-2

Instructional Strategies Development Sheet (continued)

5. Synthesis

5.1 Organize information from multiple sources.
5.2 Present information.

6. Evaluation

6.1 Judge the product (effectiveness).
6.2 Judge the information problem-solving process (efficiency).

Developing Big6™ Understandings: Worksheet 6-3

Curriculum Situations	Big6 Connection

Collaboration: Partnerships for Instructional Improvement

By Bob Berkowitz, with Max Stoner and John DonVito

[Editor's Note: The example used in this article is a collaborative unit developed for tenth graders. However, thc unit may easily be modified for lower grade levels and, more importantly, it is only an example that is used to illustrate the collaborative process.]

The value of an integrated approach to library and information skills instruction in undeniable. It promotes cooperative planning between teachers and library media specialists, and commitment to joint goals and objectives. It is through the integrated instructional model that the content curriculum and library and information problem solving skills are linked to provide meaningful information skills instruction. However, in order to implement the integrated model effectively and gain maximum benefits, both teachers and library media specialists face two problems:

1. How to select the best opportunities within the content curriculum scope and sequence with which to integrate, and
2. How to design instructional units that motivate students to learn and use information problem-solving skills effectively.

Teachers are undoubtedly the best source of information regarding the taught curriculum—the content and structure, the scope and sequence of what really goes on in the classroom. Teachers are able to ensure that the content and timing of the instructional unit is appropriate and meets the needs of students. A library media specialist, acting in the instructional-consultant role, can ensure that the instructional unit integrates library and information skills in ways that are involving, challenging, and meaningful to students. Additionally, library media specialists can provide a school-wide perspective of the information skills that need to be taught or reviewed as necessary. Teachers and library media specialists, acting collaboratively, can explore a range of creative and logical learning experiences, and design instructional units that teach, remediate, or review content and information skills. Understanding the roles that both teachers and library media specialists play is only the first step to successful collaborative efforts. Ultimately, the willingness of teachers and library media specialists to involve themselves actively in the collaborative design of instruction units is essential to success. Initial success builds partners for continued collaborative efforts.

One such collaborative effort, "Renaissance to Industrialization: A Social, Political, and Economic Comparison," is a tenth grade Global Studies unit based on the Big Six Skills © (Eisenberg and Berkowitz, 1990) approach to information skills instruction, which meets the twofold challenge of timing and motivation. Our previous experiences at collaboration had focused on enhancing the quality of existing classroom activities and student achievement. By analyzing instruction, content, and student performance from an information problem-solving perspective, we redesigned the existing course content to incorporate information problem-solving skills. The results of this effort were that students were more confident in their ability to use content information to complete assignments. This was reflected both in the quality of the products and presentations as well as in test scores. We had realized our goals. Based on this success, we were eager to try our hand a t designing an integrated unit that would extend our instructional program in Global Studies. We decided to try something not usually viewed as an obvious target to integration with library and information skills instruction, to develop a unit that would review and remediate content. The result is the unit described below, and included in this article.

"Renaissance to Industrialization: A Social, Political and Economic Comparison" is taught at the end of the first semester as an opportunity for students to review and relearn 350 years of history within a two-week period. The motivational strategy that we decided to use was to incorporate student interest in role-playing games and family history with small-group work and multiple presentation opportunities in order to have students use information in a variety of ways. Given this set of parameters, we took what we believe is an interesting (if not unique) approach. As you read through the unit, we hope it is obvious that it capitalizes on its ability to release students' imaginations. And, through its variety of presentation modes, it affords students multiple opportunities to exhibit this command of the content information.

For an information-skills perspective, the Big Six Skills © focus this unit is on Task Definition, Information Use, Synthesis, and Evaluation. Students are engaged in important skills activities, including:

- understanding and explaining the requirements of the assignment,
- determining the information needs,
- reading for content
- selecting and summarizing useful information,
- organizing information for a variety of presentations,
- listening for a purpose, and
- assessing the presentations.

All these, of course, while students are reviewing and relearning the significant events, people, and concepts that comprise 350 years of history.

Some of the management and organizational keys that made this instructional unit successful for our students included:

- clearly defining our expectations to students,
- systematically breaking down tasks into manageable parts and monitoring students' work daily,
- carefully determining the student mix for each of the small groups, by considering learning styles, ability, personality
- continually providing clear feedback and direction from the teacher, and

- enthusiastically encouraging students to engage history and explore "their" past.

Throughout the collaborative process, each of us was committed to creating an instructional unit in which students would have a successful experience, one characterized by cooperation, respect for each other' ideas and opinions, and a positive attitude to a new approach to teaching and learning social studies. We were pleased with students' eager participation and the quality of their presentations. Each member of each small group was able to contribute to the success of the entire group. The discussion of content took place as students helped each other review and relearn the historical facts and their implications. Students were involved in discussing history as cause and effect, and had a "personal" interest in how events, people, and concepts affected "their family." Other benefits included the chance to practice communication skills that resulted from the sharing among students groups and the opportunity for students to present their ideas orally and visually, All in all, we had improved the quality of the time students spent immersed in learning history.

We urge you to adopt (or adapt0 this unit for use with your social studies teachers and students. It is easy to personalize this unit to fit your own situation. Although we used this particular unit with tenth grade, the idea is applicable to a range of grade levels. Additionally, it is possible to add to any of the activities by either extending the ones we have developed or by incorporating new activities, perhaps a student-designed timeline or a videotaped project. Another way to localize this unit is to adopt its basic instructional strategy and structure but change the time period, or region. For example, a similar unit might be designed around the time period from the Civil War to the Civil Rights Movement.

The benefit to students was great, and they are now eager to experiment with new ways of learning history and to participate in activities we are currently creating in new instructional units. The benefit for the three of us was equally great. We each have a renewed appreciation of the others' roles in the design and implementation of quality learning experiences for students.

Eisenberg, Michael B. and Berkowitz, Robert E. Information Problem-Solving: The Big Six Skills Approach to Library and Information Skills Instruction. Norwood, NJ: Ablex 1990.

Unit: Renaissance to Industrialization: A Social, Political, and Economic Comparison

Audience: Global Studies (Grade 10)

Overview: This unit of instruction gives students the opportunity to review 350 years of history from a variety of perspectives. Social, political, and economic changes that occurred in England from 1500 to 1850 are the focus. The device used to meet this goal and stimulate student interest is the concept of family history. Students, working cooperatively in small groups, are required to assume that they are people living in England in 1850. Their task is to create a "family tree" of direct descendents dating back to 1500. Additionally, students are required to write a short family history and present an oral portrait of two family members from each century. As part of the family history, students are required to incorporate tow significant historical events or concepts, and two historical personalities, as well as comment on the impact of one social, one political, and one economic issue for each family member "portrait."

Rationale: It is important for students to be able to trace the changes in major historical themes (social, political, economic influences) as a means to understanding history. Additionally, this project acts as a review, remediation, and reinforcement exercise.

Subject Area Objectives: The major objectives to be covered in this unit of study include, but are not limited to:

Social: Students will demonstrate their understanding of:

- the movement of large portions of the population from farms to cities.
- how living and working conditions changed.
- the effect of religious intolerance and the impact of religious affiliation on daily life.
- the changes in culture (e.g., the ideas that characterized Renaissance thought).
- the distribution of wealth.
- the reasons for and effects of the Reformation.
- how Enlightenment's ideas spread throughout society.
- how socialists proposed to deal with changes in society.

Political: Students will demonstrate their understanding of:

- the change from absolute monarchy to limited monarchy to constitutional state.
- the causes and effects of revolutions.
- the impact of laws (e.g., Factory Act).
- imperialism.
- role of government and its impact on daily life.
- how disagreements between kings and Parliament led to civil war.
- the aftermath of the English Civil War.

Economic: Students will demonstrate their understanding of:

- the changes that occurred in the English economy in the 1500's and 1600's.
- the growth of socialism.
- the influence of the factory system.
- how mercantilism (trade with foreign countries) changed trade and business practices.
- the effect of unionism.
- changes in personal finances.
- how England took part in exploration and trade, and the role England played in the colonization of North America.
- how Queen Elizabeth I brought prosperity to England.
- why the Industrial Revolution began in Great Britain.
- how new inventions and methods of production helped to transform industry.

Big Six Objectives:

Task Definition: Students will demonstrate the ability to:
- explain the requirements of the assignment.
- create questions to research.

Information Use: Students will demonstrate the ability to:
- select appropriate information.
- acquire information from a variety of sources.
- summarize information.

Synthesis: Students will demonstrate the ability to:
- prepare a "family tree" (visual).
- prepare "family portraits" report (written).
- make class presentations (oral).

Evaluation: Students will demonstrate the ability to:
- assess products (visual, written, oral) based on the evaluation criteria.
- assess classmates' oral presentations based on criteria given.
- convey appropriate information accurately.
- convey accurate information appropriately.

Materials:

"Significant Events, Concepts, and People" Sheet
"Information about the Characters" Sheet
Examples of family trees
Examples of family histories / chronicles / diaries
"Audience Information Collection and Evaluation" Sheets
Peer Evaluation Sheets

Significant Events, Concepts, and People

1500s (Examples)

Sea Dogs	Phillip II of Spain
Act of Supremacy	Henry VIII
Raleigh settles Roanoke	Harvey
Elizabeth becomes Queen	Thomas More
Bloody Mary is Queen	Sir Francis Drake
War of Roses	John Hawkins
Spanish Armada	Henry VII
Guilds	Jane Seymour
Plague	Prince Edward
Elizabeth I	

1600s (Examples)

Puritan Revolution	Shakespeare
Glorious Revolution	Cromwell
Etc.	

1700s (Examples)

American Revolution	George III
Prime Minister	Walpole
Etc.	

1800s (Example)

Act of Union	Tennyson
Urbanization	Keats
Etc.	

Information about the Characters

General Knowledge: As you read about the characters in this role-playing simulation, it is important to know that one characteristic that each of these people have in common is that from one generation to the next, the family occupation has generally remained similar. In those instances in which occupations did change, the change was as the result of social, political, or economic facts that impacted the family. If that occurred within the family history of your character, you will need to indicate the event or situation that accounts for the change in occupation.

Curator of Westminster Abbey and Windsor Castle

Edmond Crenshire is a member of the wealthy class. He maintains church records and art treasures of the realm. He is directly responsible to the Archbishop of Canterbury. Edmond Crenshire is a crotchety old geezer who hates change. He has been the Curator for more than 40 years. He is interested in the arts and especially literature. He meets regularly with representatives of the Archbishop. Edmond is keenly aware of the power of the written word. He was a regular visitor at the court of King George III.

Factory Worker

Lydia's grandmother and grandfather lived on a farm in rural Yorkshire. Now, however, she is working in a factory in Leeds. She is concerned about her family and unionism. Lydia is 37 years old. She lives with her husband who is also a factory worker and their six children, ages three to fourteen. One of her children, a daughter age ten, died two years ago in a factory accident.

Factory Owner

Arthur Newbury is owner of a textile factory that makes cotton yard goods. He is concerned about overseas trace, decreasing profits, and the growth of socialism. A member of a men's club, he is adamant in his opposition to government interference and, for that matter, any laws that will give workers rights. He is in favor of a laissez-faire approach to government. He lives with his wife and four children in Manchester.

Scientist/Inventor

Jonathan Smyth is a free-thinking individual whose background is blacksmithing and tinsmithing. Lately, he has been experimenting with something he calls the "puddling process." He is a friend of Mr. Bessimer. Mr. Smyth, who is only 36 years old, is not married, and can devote much of his time to designing machine parts for factory equipment and creating new types of machinery to increase textile production.

Member of the House of Lords

Sir Reginald Appleton's main concern is maintaining the power of the wealthy and nobility. He is a member of the Anglican Church. Sir Reginald's family has held a seat in the House of Lords since the 1300s. He lives in a manor house in Lands End with his wife, five children (four daughters and a son age 12), and a number of servants.

Member of the House of Commons

James Tewkson is a Puritan. James is concerned about the working conditions in factories. Additionally, he is concerned with other social issues such as health and morality. He was elected by the people of Kent, a Borough outside of London James. Like his father before him, he is a barrister of some financial means.

Merchant

Charles Crawford owns a women's clothing store in Manchester. His primary customers are wealthy women. His store is a center for gossip among wealthy women. Keeping his ear open to his customers' conversations for more than their fashion likes and dislikes, he also can keep tabs on the latest political and economic issues of the day. Charles invests his considerable profits in overseas trading.

Naval Officer

Richard Seaforth is a captain in the Royal Navy. His present commission is as Captain of the Frigate Rockingham. Richard's father was also a navy man. When Richard was seven years old, his father was able to get his son a situation as a cabinboy. The Seaforth family lives in Liverpool. Richard spends from eight-ten months at a time at sea. He is well read, and spends much of his time reading the history of great naval battles. Richard once met men who served on the frigate Macedonian. Captain Seaforth is anxious to transfer to an expeditionary force.

Information Use Plan for "Family Portrait"		
Date	**Events/Concepts**	**People**
Social		
Political		
Economic		
As a group, research all of the events/concepts and choose which ones to include in each written portrait. Use the "Impact" sheet to record your information.		

Impact of Events/Concepts and People x Century

Event:

____

____

____

Concept:

____

____

____

Person:

____

____

____

Audience Information Collection and Evaluation Sheet

Other than your own group, which group made the most accurate presentation of the social, political, and economic changes which occured from 1500-1850? Explain your decision.

Activities:

1. Introduction to the project and its requirements. Students will be divided into small groups and assigned "characters." Each group will research events / concepts and people (see list).
2. Teacher will define "family tree" as a graphic representation that shows relationships among family members in and across generations. Students will be shown sample "family trees" and directed in a brainstorming session to determine creative and alternative ways of graphically representing family history.
3. Working in small groups, students will begin to develop their "family trees."
4. Students will begin the process of researching the background of each family member about whom they choose to write. Students will complete the "family portrait by person" plan.
5. Teachers will review the requirements for the written "family portrait" / biography. Students continue to meet in small groups (and work individually) to develop their "family history," design their graphic presentation, and continue their research.
6. Students display "family trees."
7. Students present oral report (20 minutes for each group including question-and-answer period). Students in audience complete "audience information collection and evaluation" sheet.
8. Students submit all written work as well as graphic representation.

Evaluation:

General Guidelines: Students will receive group grades. Each group will be graded based on the following criteria:

Completeness of Plan—20%
- including: the required amount of information, its accuracy and appropriateness

Oral Presentation—20%
- including: accuracy, appropriateness and completeness of the information

Evaluation—20%
- based on: peer evaluation comments

Family Tree and Written Report—40%
- based on: completeness, accuracy in the use of appropriate information.

Peer Evaluation Sheet

		Events/ Concepts	People	Explain why you think the character was/ wasn't consistent with the times.
Character	**Social**	1 2 Impact	1 2 Impact	
Date	**Political**	1 2 Impact	1 2 Impact	
Person	**Economic**	1 2 Impact	1 2 Impact	

This article is reprinted with publisher's permission.

Berkowitz, R. E., Stoner, M., & DonVito, J. (1994). Collaboration: Partnerships for instructional improvement. *School Library Media Activities Monthly, 10*(7), 32-35.

Call to Action: Getting Serious about Libraries and Information in Education

by Mike Eisenberg
Director, University of Washington School of Library and Information Science

and Carrie Lowe
ERIC Clearinghouse on Information Technology, Syracuse University

MultiMedia Schools • March/April 1999
Copyright 1999, Information Today, Inc.

[Editor's Note: You may remember from your schooling the image of the FireTriangle. Fire can be sustained only when there is fuel, oxygen, and heat. As you'll see below, achieving technology's potential for learning requires a similar set of conditions. Evaluated, organized content is the fuel (provided by Library/Media specialists); carefully planned instructional experiences is the oxygen (provided by classroom teachers); the commitment and energy to make things happen is the heat (provided by administrators). Firefighters know that all it takes to extinguish a fire is to break the link between any of these three elements. We need to be fire builders who can spark the flame of lifelong learning, and the following feature challenges us to begin.]

The work of the Information & Technology team goes beyond creating technology-rich learning environment for students, ...

The Information & Technology Team

In the past few years, we've had the opportunity to work with educators and communities across the U.S. and all over the world. In that time, we've seen some highly effective information and technology programs, and others that are...uh, frankly less than effective. Why do some schools and districts thrive in terms of meaningful integration of technology with learning and teaching while others do not?

This, of course, is a complicated question. There are many factors that contribute to the successful use of technology in education, including:

- vision and clear setting of goals and objectives
- training and continuous support for teachers
- systematic and continuous planning, evaluation, and revision.

However, in our experience, there is one aspect of successful technology deployment that is even more important than all of these together—teamwork. We're not talking about a general, pollyanna-ish, "let's all work together" approach to teamwork. We are talking about a true integration of information, library, and instructional technology services, systems, resources and roles in a unified Information & Technology team.

The members of the Information & Technology team can be found within your own school: technology teachers, library and information professionals, and key administrators. All you need to add is commitment, enthusiasm, and teamwork. A unified I&T team is one in which team members work together to provide services and resources to classroom teachers, students, and even parents. Schools with strong, committed I&T teams invariably see great results in their schools, and not only in terms of what their students are learning. These collaborative programs enjoy excellent funding, the respect of their colleagues, and influence over administrative decisions.

The work of the Information & Technology team goes beyond creating technology-rich learning environment for students, although this is one of their most important tasks. Great I&T teams have a close relationship with classroom teachers and administration, and their responsibilities affect every aspect of the school. They provide a technical support system by coordinating tech services and resources and coordinating purchasing decisions. In terms of curriculum, the I&T team oversees the information and technology literacy program and ensures that it is implemented as part of the classroom curriculum. An active, dynamic Information & Technology team is an integral part of the school; the team is the right arm of overburdened administrators and teachers.

Unfortunately, at this time, we don't see enough of these I&T teams in schools and districts. Too often we see library media specialists, technology teachers, and administrators working in isolation and fighting for turf and control. At the same time, these educators bemoan their feelings of professional disenfranchisement, their inability to interest colleagues in collaboration, being overwhelmed with just too much to do, and worst of all, budget cuts and eliminated positions. Although they all say that they are working toward a common goal—preparing students for success in the information age—they are not working together.

Is it possible for library media specialists and technology teachers to work together with administrators and other educators? It is not simply possible, it is necessary that they do so in order to become the active players in curriculum and instruction that they must be in the coming decades to ensure the success of students in the information age.

The Technology Question

The 1957 Katherine Hepburn and Spencer Tracy movie Desk Set tells the story of several librarians working in the research department of a newspaper whose jobs are threatened by the arrival of a computer designed to do their jobs better and faster. This suspicion of technology has not changed in the last 40 years; indeed, many of us, both teachers and library media specialists, dread the day that we are replaced by computers.

This is far from an irrational fear. For many of us, our first introduction to the idea of computers in the classroom came the day machines were wheeled into our classroom and dumped in the corner. This is a blatant intrusion onto our turf. We hear of other jobs, such as those in manufacturing, being replaced more and more by computers. Who hasn't looked in the corner of the classroom and imagined the computers sitting there one day sitting on top of the desk you currently occupy at the front of the room, conducting the class?

Can library media specialists, technology teachers, and classroom teachers be replaced by technology? Absolutely not. We believe just the opposite. Library and information technology professionals are the true innovators of using technology to facilitate learning. As technology becomes more prevalent in learning and teaching, there is even greater need for information, library, and technology work in schools. This is a role that librarians can and must assume to create information-literate students.

The word "disintermediation" is batted around quite a bit in reference to future technologies. Disintermediation is the idea that as technology becomes more advanced, users will no longer require assistance to use it. The development of the World Wide Web has told a very different story. We have seen a staggering rise in the use of question-and-answer services (such as AskERIC, the question-and-answer service for education) in the past five years. As the Web becomes larger and more tangled, users need help finding what they want. This is where information and technology specialists step in.

The Key Is Teamwork

While our skills and strengths make us, as members of the Information & Technology team, the logical choice to lead students, teachers, and administrators into the information age, we cannot expect to have leadership roles handed to us. In order to take advantage of the opportunities awaiting us, it is necessary for us to reinvent ourselves. We cannot just expect to give our students more of the same in the next years; the changes in store for teaching and learning promise to be too profound.

We must reinvent ourselves as a dynamic, flexible team. It is impossible for any one of us—teachers and administrators, library media specialists, or technology teachers—to handle every responsibility the school of the future will present. To create the technology-rich learning center of the future, we need full partnership and true integration of responsibilities. By joining forces, we can share our strengths and assume a leadership role in schools and districts feeling the pressures of technology.

Facing the Challenge

No one is really sure what the school of the future will look like. We do know that it is going to be different, and a lot of that difference is going to be due to the influx of technology into classrooms and learning centers. This uncertainty means that library media specialists, technology teachers, and administrators must work together to answer three key questions: What needs to be done? Who will do it? Finally, how will it be done? These are the questions addressed here.

What needs to be done?

This question is deceptively simple. The first answer that comes to mind is "to integrate technology into learning and teaching." However, this is tantamount to not seeing the forest for the proverbial trees. It is key to remember why parents, school boards, and politicians are supplying us with computers for our schools and demanding that we use them.

The reason is, of course, that we are preparing students for a future that is very different from the one we faced as graduates. Even lower-level employment will demand familiarity and ability to work with technology. For this reason, it is essential that we give students the tools and skills which will allow them to be successful in tomorrow's workplace.

What needs to be done goes beyond sitting students in front of a computer and showing them how to turn on the machine. We must work together with our colleagues to prepare students for the technology-rich workplace they will face in the future.

How will it be done?

When strategizing with other educators about how to best prepare students, it is imperative to remember that we are preparing students for the technologies of tomorrow, not those of today. This means that we must teach students strategies and ways of thinking about technology, rather than discrete skill sets. After all, skills become obsolete when the technology they relate to becomes obsolete.

The key to equipping students with the skills that they will need to succeed in the future lies in information and technology literacy instruction. The new standards for library media programs, Information Power, defines information literacy as "the ability to find and use information" (AASL/AECT, p. 1). It goes on to say, "Students must become skillful consumers and producers of information in a range of sources and formats to thrive personally and economically in the information age" (p. 2). To create information-literate students, educators must concentrate on processes (such as information problem solving and critical thinking skills) rather than computer skills.

Students must be taught that technology is a tool, rather than an answer in and of itself. Teach students that there are three uses of technology in a modern society—information technology (such as electronic resources), communication technology (telecommunications), and processing technology (software that helps us do better, faster work). Once students recognize that technology is a means to an end, they will be well on their way to being information-literate, productive citizens of a future society.

We teach technology skills within the overall information problem-solving process using the Eisenberg and Berkowitz Big6 Skills approach (see the Big6 Web site—http://big6.com). The Big6 is a tried and proven method of teaching information and technology skills in context (see Eisenberg and Johnson, 1996). The Big6 can be considered from a number of perspectives—as an information and technology literacy curriculum, an information problem-solving process, a set of skills for effectively and efficiently meeting information needs, and an overall method for developing programs to help students learn essential information and technology skills.

Who will do it?

Preparing students for a technology-rich society that is unlike anything we have ever known is a tall order. It requires leadership, imagination, and hard work. To fulfill this mission, we need the skills and talents of all three members of the Information & Technology team: the technology teacher to implement and support instructional technology, the library media specialist to work with teachers to create information- and technology-rich curriculum, and the administrator to follow through and put plans into action .

However, the Information & Technology team cannot work alone. Team members must be sure that they are constantly communicating with classroom teachers, administrators, and school policy-makers to ensure that they are doing their job. If others are not included in important decisions to some extent, it is less likely that they will buy into resulting change.

At this point, we must proudly admit our biases. As librarians, we think that it is impossible to successfully prepare students for the information age without the help of the library and information professional. The skill of the librarian lies in finding exactly what is needed in a glut of information. This ability to look critically at information is an essential component of information and technology literacy.

The library and information professional brings the "information" component to the Information & Technology team. Information is a librarian's business, and librarians are most qualified to create and assist teachers in implementing information literacy instruction. In terms of technology, librarians have led the way in teaching students technology skills in context throughout their professional history.

Clearly, the library and information professional is an essential component of the Information & Technology team. At the same time, we must stress the necessity for librarians to reinvent themselves as they face new professional challenges. It is key that every library media specialist who is serious about preparing students for the information age read Information Power and follow its directives for becoming dynamic, active information professionals.

[Editor's Note: I've found the Big6 Newsletter to be an invaluable resource for visions, strategies, and tools to teach essential skills for the information age. See http://www.big6.com/newsletter/index.html.]

A "Call to Action"

Gary Hartzell, former school administrator, prolific author, and professor of education at the University of Nebraska, spoke recently at the Washington Library Media Association Conference. In his presentation, Hartzell pointed out that no course in any major school of education in this country focuses on the use of library and information in learning and teaching. He went on to say that in almost all teacher training programs, there is little mention of the role of the library media program and the library and information professional at all. You can be sure that the Information & Technology team suffers from the same lack of recognition.

Therefore, we end this article with a "call to action." It's similar to the one that we sent to LM_NET, the library media mailing list. What if ... we all pledged to actively spread the word about the importance of information, libraries, and technology in learning and teaching? We know that everyone is busy and can't even keep up. But what if we did this anyway?

What if each of us dedicated ourselves to communicating to a wide audience the importance of information, libraries, and technology in learning and teaching? Information Power states that our mission is "to ensure that students and staff are effective users of ideas and information." Isn't it time we explained what this really means and how we must work together to make it so?

One clear way is that library and information professionals, technology teachers, and administrators must market themselves as the Information & Technology team. This message must be directed at schools of education and teacher training programs. This is a task we must undertake for the future of learning and teaching. We must get in touch with the local university and volunteer to speak in teacher training classes. We must lobby for a course on information, information literacy, and information technology (or volunteer to teach it ourselves). If new teachers and administrators have no training in use of libraries and information in their schools, how can we expect them to change? This is our first (and perhaps most important) task as the Information & Technology team of tomorrow.

References

American Association of School Librarians and Association for Educational Communications and Technology (1998). *Information Power: Building Partnerships for Learning.* Chicago: American Library Association.

Eisenberg, M. and Berkowitz, R. (1998) "The Big6 Skills," http://big6.com

Eisenberg, M. and Johnson, D.(1996). Computer Skills for Information Problem-Solving: Learning and Teaching Technology in Context," *ERIC Digest*. Syracuse, NY: ERIC Clearinghouse on Information & Technology. Available online at http://ericir.syr.edu/ithome/digests/computerskills.html

Communications to the authors may be directed to:

Dr. Michael B. Eisenberg, Director, University of Washington School of Library and Information Science, Box 352930, Seattle, WA 98195-2930; 206/543-1794; e-mail: mbe@u.washington.edu

Carrie Lowe, Gateway to Educational Materials Project Representative, ERIC Clearinghouse on Information & Technology, 4-194 Center for Science and Technology, Syracuse University, Syracuse, NY 13244-4100; 315/443-3640; e-mail: calowe@ericir.syr.edu

---

This article is reprinted with the publisher's permission.

Eisenberg, M. E., & Lowe, C. (1999). Call to action: Getting serious about libraries and information education. *MultiMedia Schools, 6*(2), 18-21.

Think Sheet

Part VII:

Curriculum Mapping

Introduction

In Part IV, we noted that there are two levels of instructional design: micro and macro. In that section, we focused on the micro level in terms of lesson and unit design. Here, we go deeper into ways of implementing the Big6 on the macro level. The intent is to facilitate integration of information skills instruction on the classroom, school, district, region, or even state level.

We continually stress that Big6 instruction is fully compatible with existing subject area and classroom curriculum. The Big6 provides students with the information understandings and skills necessary to carry out the various learning tasks provided by curriculum standards and frameworks. However, to successfully integrate Big6 instruction requires accurate, up-to-date, and specific information about the curriculum on classroom, school, or district levels. In essence, we have an information problem of our own to solve—what is the "real" curriculum taught to students? We use the "Curriculum-Related Information Resources Brainstorming Sheet" provided in this section to brainstorm information seeking alternatives for curriculum information.

For example, school, district, or state curriculum guides are widely available sources of curriculum information. They provide some degree of detail on the curriculum as intended, but they do not provide specifics of the actual curriculum as experienced by students and teachers. Textbooks and websites may also provide usable curriculum information.

Since the mid-1970s, Mike has used a technique called "curriculum mapping" to gather, organize, and present reliable curriculum information. Curriculum mapping provides a mechanism for gathering specific and accurate information on the various attributes of classroom curriculum. The primary building block of curriculum in K–12 schools is the curriculum unit. Therefore, curriculum mapping is based on gathering data—generally from teachers, but sometimes from students—about actual curriculum units or units intended for teaching.

Curriculum mapping involves two steps:

1. Systematically collecting information about what's actually going on in the classroom, and
2. Combining this information into charts and tables that describe the curriculum in a particular setting.

The "Curriculum Mapping Data Collection Worksheet" is the primary tool for gathering data on curriculum units. Multiple copies are provided so that audiences can experience the ease of filling out one or two and still have some left over. It only takes 5 to 10 minutes to complete a Curriculum Mapping Data Collection Worksheet. The Curriculum Mapping Data Collection Worksheet has undergone dozens of revisions over the years and should be individualized to local school settings. *To save time and effort, no data should be gathered that is already available.* School name, for example, should be already listed on the form, and the terms used to describe various teaching methods and assignments should reflect local vocabulary.

The Curriculum Mapping Data Collection Worksheet itself is not a curriculum map. A curriculum map is the compiled information from multiple Worksheets. A blank form is provided to create a curriculum map, but this can also be accomplished using a computer database or electronic spreadsheet program. We also provide numerous examples of curriculum maps to show the usefulness and flexibility of the technique on the classroom, school, subject area, and district level as well as across grade levels—elementary, middle, and high school.

Once maps are created, the task is to use the information in curriculum maps for planning Big6 instruction that is integrated with classroom, subject area curriculum. Planning integrated instruction involves systematically reviewing the curriculum maps and selecting units that are best suited to integrated information and technology skills instruction. What we are trying to do is to identify the "big juicy" units, those information-rich curriculum units which are filled with information needs, resources, and processing. These are the units that offer particularly good opportunities for teaching specific Big6 Skills within the overall Big6 process.

For example, units that are good candidates for integrating Big6 Skills instruction generally:

- Have a longer duration
- Involve a report, project, or product rather than a quiz or test
- Use multiple resources
- Involve a range of teaching methods.

Once desirable units are selected, they can be entered into the Big6 Skills by Unit Matrix. If developed at the beginning of the school year, the Big6 Skills by Unit Matrix becomes a blueprint for integrated information skills instruction. It can also be updated during the year to reflect what actually takes place. Finally, at the end of the year, the Matrix offers detailed documentation of what was actually accomplished. The Matrix also serves as the basis for follow-up planning by the teacher for the next year *and* for other teachers who will have the same students the next year.

Skills by Unit matrices can be created for individual teachers, teams, subject areas, schools, or even districts. Examples of various matrices are provided.

We cannot over-emphasize the importance of teaching all skills in context. The process of systematically reviewing curriculum, identifying valuable units for integrated instruction, and developing and documenting plans is important to a successful Big6 program. The tools provided here give educators practical means for accomplishing meaningful, integrated Big6—classroom curriculum instruction.

Overview

Information & Technology Skills for Student Success: The Big6™ Skills Approach

Curriculum Contexts

- Math class working on graphs
- Social Studies discussion of current issues
- Science lab or projects
- English writing and vocabulary
- Health reports

- Any assignment, particularly a project, report, or paper!!

- Any personal decision that calls for information, e.g., selecting a TV show, buying a product...

Curriculum Information—Information Seeking Strategies: Worksheet 7-1

Determine All Possible Sources	Select Best Sources

Integrating into the Curriculum: Curriculum Mapping
Data Collection Worksheet 7-2

School:	

Date:	

Grade:	
Teacher:	
Subject:	
Unit:	

Number of Sections:	
Number of Students:	
Total Teaching Time:	
Marking Period:	

Level of Instruction:
- introduced
- reinforced
- expanded

Comment:

Resources:
- text
- one source
- multiple sources
  - reference (print/electr.)
  - periodicals
  - WWW
  - book (nonfiction)
  - book (fiction)
  - human
  - other:

Organization of Instruction
- large group
- small group
- individual

Comment:

Primary Teaching Method
- desk work
- lecture
- demonstration
- video, film, multimedia
- lab, hands-on
- discussion
- independent study
- multimedia project
- report
- other:

Assignment(s):
- test
- short written assignment
- report
- project/product
- observation
- other:

Technologies:
- **tool** (word processing, database, presentation, spreadsheet)
- **communication** (e-mail, listserv, chat, video conferencing)
- **information** (web, database, electronic resources, Q&A)
- other:

Big6:
- Task Definition
- Information Seeking Strategies
- Location & Access
- Use of Information
- Synthesis
- Evaluation

Library & Information Services:
- resources provision
- facilities provision (incl technology)
- reading guidance
- information service
- skills instruction (direct, indirect)
- consultation

Comments:

Eisenberg/Berkowitz, January 1998

Integrating into the Curriculum: Curriculum Mapping Data Collection Worksheet 7-2

School:		*Date:*	

Grade:		*Number of Sections:*	
Teacher:		*Number of Students:*	
Subject:		*Total Teaching Time:*	
Unit:		*Marking Period:*	

Level of Instruction:
- introduced
- reinforced
- expanded

Comment:

Resources:
- text
- one source
- multiple sources
  - reference (print/electr.)
  - periodicals
  - WWW
  - book (nonfiction)
  - book (fiction)
  - human
  - other:

Organization of Instruction
- large group
- small group
- individual

Comment:

Primary Teaching Method
- desk work
- lecture
- demonstration
- video, film, multimedia
- lab, hands-on
- discussion
- independent study
- multimedia project
- report
- other:

Assignment(s):
- test
- short written assignment
- report
- project/product
- observation
- other:

Technologies:
- **tool** (word processing, database, presentation, spreadsheet)
- **communication** (e-mail, listserv, chat, video conferencing)
- **information** (web, database, electronic resources, Q&A)
- other:

Big6:
- Task Definition
- Information Seeking Strategies
- Location & Access
- Use of Information
- Synthesis
- Evaluation

Library & Information Services:
- resources provision
- facilities provision (incl technology)
- reading guidance
- information service
- skills instruction (direct, indirect)
- consultation

Comments:

Eisenberg/Berkowitz, January 1998

Integrating into the Curriculum: Curriculum Mapping
Data Collection Worksheet 7-2

School:	

Date:	

Grade:	
Teacher:	
Subject:	
Unit:	

Number of Sections:	
Number of Students:	
Total Teaching Time:	
Marking Period:	

Level of Instruction:
- introduced
- reinforced
- expanded

Comment:

Resources:
- text
- one source
- multiple sources
  - reference (print/electr.)
  - periodicals
  - WWW
  - book (nonfiction)
  - book (fiction)
  - human
  - other:

Organization of Instruction
- large group
- small group
- individual

Comment:

Primary Teaching Method
- desk work
- lecture
- demonstration
- video, film, multimedia
- lab, hands-on
- discussion
- independent study
- multimedia project
- report
- other:

Assignment(s):
- test
- short written assignment
- report
- project/product
- observation
- other:

Technologies:
- **tool** (word processing, database, presentation, spreadsheet)
- **communication** (e-mail, listserv, chat, video conferencing)
- **information** (web, database, electronic resources, Q&A)
- other:

Big6:
- Task Definition
- Information Seeking Strategies
- Location & Access
- Use of Information
- Synthesis
- Evaluation

Library & Information Services:
- resources provision
- facilities provision (incl technology)
- reading guidance
- information service
- skills instruction (direct, indirect)
- consultation

Comments:

Eisenberg/Berkowitz, January 1998

Integrating into the Curriculum: Curriculum Mapping Data Collection Worksheet 7-2

School:	

Date:	

Grade:	
Teacher:	
Subject:	
Unit:	

Number of Sections:	
Number of Students:	
Total Teaching Time:	
Marking Period:	

Level of Instruction:
- introduced
- reinforced
- expanded

Comment:

Assignment(s):
- test
- short written assignment
- report
- project/product
- observation
- other:

Resources:
- text
- one source
- multiple sources
  - reference (print/electr.)
  - periodicals
  - WWW
  - book (nonfiction)
  - book (fiction)
  - human
  - other:

Technologies:
- **tool** (word processing, database, presentation, spreadsheet)
- **communication** (e-mail, listserv, chat, video conferencing)
- **information** (web, database, electronic resources, Q&A)
- other:

Organization of Instruction
- large group
- small group
- individual

Comment:

Big6:
- Task Definition
- Information Seeking Strategies
- Location & Access
- Use of Information
- Synthesis
- Evaluation

Primary Teaching Method
- desk work
- lecture
- demonstration
- video, film, multimedia
- lab, hands-on
- discussion
- independent study
- multimedia project
- report
- other:

Library & Information Services:
- resources provision
- facilities provision (incl technology)
- reading guidance
- information service
- skills instruction (direct, indirect)
- consultation

Comments:

Eisenberg/Berkowitz, January 1998

Integrating into the Curriculum: Curriculum Mapping Data Collection Worksheet 7-2

School:	

Date:	

Grade:	
Teacher:	
Subject:	
Unit:	

Number of Sections:	
Number of Students:	
Total Teaching Time:	
Marking Period:	

Level of Instruction:
- introduced
- reinforced
- expanded

Comment:

Resources:
- text
- one source
- multiple sources
  - reference (print/electr.)
  - periodicals
  - WWW
  - book (nonfiction)
  - book (fiction)
  - human
  - other:

Organization of Instruction
- large group
- small group
- individual

Comment:

Primary Teaching Method
- desk work
- lecture
- demonstration
- video, film, multimedia
- lab, hands-on
- discussion
- independent study
- multimedia project
- report
- other:

Assignment(s):
- test
- short written assignment
- report
- project/product
- observation
- other:

Technologies:
- **tool** (word processing, database, presentation, spreadsheet)
- **communication** (e-mail, listserv, chat, video conferencing)
- **information** (web, database, electronic resources, Q&A)
- other:

Big6:
- Task Definition
- Information Seeking Strategies
- Location & Access
- Use of Information
- Synthesis
- Evaluation

Library & Information Services:
- resources provision
- facilities provision (incl technology)
- reading guidance
- information service
- skills instruction (direct, indirect)
- consultation

Comments:

Eisenberg/Berkowitz, January 1998

Integrating into the Curriculum: Curriculum Mapping

Curriculum Map

GR	TCHR	SUBJ	UNIT	#SEC	#STUD	TIME	MAR_PER	LEV	RES	ORG	METHODS	ASSIGN	TECH	Big6	SERV	DATE

Integrating into the Curriculum: Curriculum Mapping

Sample Curriculum Map - All Fields Sorted by GR, SUBJ, MAR_P

GR	TCHR	SUBJ	UNIT	#SEC	#STUD	TIME	MAR_PER	LEV	RES	ORG	METHODS	ASSIGN	TECH	Big6	SERV	DATE
00-00	LIE	LA	Colors	1	24	40	1234	I	mult	lg	disc/hands-on	worksheet	none			01/03/98
01-01	REB	LA	ABC book	1	25	15	x2xx	R/E	mult	lg/ind	demo/ind study	product	none			01/03/98
01-01	MAB	Math	Whole/Parts	1	32	10	x2xx	I	text/mult	lg	lect/desk work	worksheet	none			01/03/98
03-03	RDY	Sci	Planets	1	33	15	xx3x	I	mult	sg/lg	lect/group	project	WWW			01/03/98
03-03	RDY	Sci	Endangered Animals	1	33	15	xxx4	I	mult	lg/ind	lect/disc/ind	project	Hyperstudio/WWW			01/03/98
03-03	RDY	SS	Community	1	33	20	x2xx	R/E	mult	sg/lg	lect/disc/trip	project	Hyperstudio			01/03/98
03-04	CAL	LA	Letter Writing	1	27	8	x2xx	I	mult	ind	lect/desk work	product	w proc			09/27/97
03-04	CAL	Math	Graphs	1	27	15	xxx4	I	test	lg/ind	lect/desk work	product	none			09/27/97
03-04	CAL	Sci	Simple Machines	1	27	40	1xxx	I/R	text/mult	sg	lab/ind study	products	none			09/27/97
03-04	CAL	Sci	Work and Energy	1	27	8	xxx4	I	text	lg	lect	text	none			09/27/97
05-05	MBE	Library	Biography	5	120	2	xx3x	R/E	mult	lg	lect/disc	none	online catalog	1 2 3	res prov	01/03/98
06-06	SEW	LA	Folktales and Legends	1	29	20	x23x	R/E	mult	lg	lect/disc/desk work	homework/test	none			01/03/98
06-06	SEW	Sci	Vocabulary	1	29	3	1xxx	R/E	text	lg/ind	lect/desk work	homework	none			01/03/98
06-06	SEW	SS	Current Events	1	29	40	1234	I/R/E	mult	lg/ind	disc/ind study	report	WWW			01/03/98
06-06	SEW	SS	Native Americans - Iroquois	1	29	10	x2xx	I	text	lg	lect/desk work	test	none			01/03/98

Integrating into the Curriculum: Curriculum Mapping

Sample Curriculum Map - All Fields Sorted by GR, SUBJ, MAR_P

GR	TCHR	SUBJ	UNIT	#SEC	#STUD	TIME	MAR_PER	LEV	RES	ORG	METHODS	ASSIGN	TECH	Big6	SERV	DATE
07-07	MBE	Library	Dictionary Skill	6	150	2	1xxx	R/E	one	lg	lect/desk work	swa	none	4		01/03/98
07-07	TMJ	Sci	Weather	3	87	15	xx3x	R/E	text	lg	lect/disc	test	none			01/03/98
07-07	TCH	SS	Recycling	3	87	15	x23x	R/E	mult	lg/ind	lect/ind	product	WWW/w proc/present/elec res, e-mail			01/03/98
08-08	TMJ	Sci	Noise	2	45	40	x2xx	R-E	mult	sg/lg/ind	demo/disc	written report	WWW/w pro/present/elec res			09/27/97
08-08	HJW	SS	Map Skills	4	111	10	1xxx	R/E	mult	lg	worksheet	worksheet	none			01/03/98
09-12	CER	Health	Diet and Nutrition	10	250	20	1x3x	R/E	mult	lg/sg	lect/disc/prod	posters	WWW/present			01/03/98
09-12	CER	Health	Tobacco and Smoking	10	250	10	1x3x	R/E	mult	lg/sg	lect/disc	test	none			01/03/98
09-12	CER	Health	Drugs	10	250	10	x2x4	R/E	mult	lg/sg	lect/disc/prod	product	WWW/present/w proc			01/03/98
10-10	MBE	Library	Web Authoring	9	20	10	x2xx	I	mult	ind	demo/prod/ind study	product (web page)	Front Page/HTML/scanner	5		09/27/97
10-10	BAB	Math	Probability	4	104	20	xx3x	R/E	text	lg/ind	lect/desk work	homework	none			01/03/98
10-12	RBW	Physics	Light Lab	1	17	4	xx3x	I/R/E	laser, lab apparatus, text	lg - pairs	lect/lab	lab report	none			09/27/97
10-12	RBW	Physics	Light	1	17	15	xx3x	I/R/E	text	lg	lect/disc	test	none			09/27/97
11-12	CJC	LA	Catcher in the Rye	3	86	10	xx3x	I	mult	lg	lect/disc	report	none			09/27/97
11-12	MAB	Spanish 4	Spanish Cooking	1	14	10	xxx4	E	mult	ind	ind	product	WWW			01/03/98
11-12	BDE	SS	Supply and Demand	3	68	20	xx3x	I/R	mult	sg/lg	lect/disc	obs/swa	none			09/27/97

Integrating into the Curriculum: Curriculum Mapping
Sample Map — Includes Some Form of Product, Project or Report

GR	TCHR	SUBJ	UNIT	#SEC	#STUD	TIME	MAR_PER	LEV	RES	ORG	METHODS	ASSIGN	TECH	Big6	SERV	DATE
01-01	REB	LA	ABC book	1	25	15	x2xx	R/E	mult	lg/ind	demo/ind study	product	none			01/03/98
03-03	RDY	Sci	Planets	1	33	15	xx3x	I	mult	sg/lg	lect/group	project	WWW			01/03/98
03-03	RDY	Sci	Endangered Animals	1	33	15	xxx4	I	mult	lg/ind	lect/disc/ind	project	Hyperstudio/WWW			01/03/98
03-03	RDY	SS	Community	1	33	20	x2xx	R/E	mult	sg/lg	lect/disc/trip	project	Hyperstudio			01/03/98
03-04	CAL	LA	Letter Writing	1	27	8	x2xx	I	mult	ind	lect/desk work	product	w proc			09/27/97
03-04	CAL	Math	Graphs	1	27	15	xxx4	I	text	lg/ind	lect/desk work	product	none			09/27/97
03-04	CAL	Sci	Simple Machines	1	27	40	1xxx	I/R	text/mult	sg	lab/ind study	products	none			09/27/97
06-06	SEW	SS	Current Events	1	29	40	1234	I/R/E	mult	lg/ind	disc/ind study	report	WWW			01/03/98
07-07	TCH	SS	Recycling	3	87	15	x23x	R/E	mult	lg/ind	lect/ind	product	WWW/w proc/present/elec res, e-mail			01/03/98
08-08	TMJ	Sci	Noise	2	45	40	x2xx	R-E	mult	sg/lg/ind	demo/disc	written report	WWW/w pro/present/elec res			09/27/97
09-12	CER	Health	Diet and Nutrition	10	250	20	1x3x	R/E	mult	lg/sg	lect/disc/prod	posters	WWW/present			01/03/98
09-12	CER	Health	Drugs	10	250	10	x2x4	R/E	mult	lg/sg	lect/disc/prod	product	WWW/present/w proc			01/03/98
10-10	MBE	Library	Web Authoring	9	20	10	x2xx	I	mult	ind	demo/prod/ind study	product (web page)	Front Page/HTML/scanner	5		09/27/97
10-12	RBW	Physics	Light Lab	1	17	4	xx3x	I/R/E	laser, lab apparatus, text	lg - pairs	lect/lab	lab report	none			09/27/97
11-12	CJC	LA	Catcher in the Rye	3	86	10	xx3x	I	mult	lg	lect/disc	report	none			09/27/97
11-12	MAB	Spanish 4	Spanish Cooking	1	14	10	xxx4	E	mult	ind	ind	product	WWW			01/03/98

Integrating into the Curriculum: Curriculum Mapping
Sample Secondary Map — Sorted by Number of Students and Time

#STUD	TIME	GR	TCHR	SUBJ	UNIT	#SEC	MAR_PER	LEV	RES	ORG	METHODS	ASSIGN	TECH	Big6	SERV	DATE
250	20	09-12	CER	Health	Diet and Nutrition	10	1x3x	R/E	mult	lg/sg	lect/disc/prod	posters	WWW/present			01/03/98
250	10	09-12	CER	Health	Tobacco and Smoking	10	1x3x	R/E	mult	lg/sg	lect/disc	test	none			01/03/98
250	10	09-12	CER	Health	Drugs	10	x2x4	R/E	mult	lg/sg	lect/disc/prod	product	WWW/present/w proc			01/03/98
150	2	07-07	MBE	Library	Dictionary Skill	6	1xxx	R/E	one	lg	lect/desk work	swa	none	4		01/03/98
111	10	08-08	HJW	SS	Map Skills	4	1xxx	R/E	mult	lg	worksheet	worksheet	none			01/03/98
104	20	10-10	BAB	Math	Probability	4	xx3x	R/E	text	lg/ind	lect/desk work	homework	none			01/03/98
87	15	07-07	TMJ	Sci	Weather	3	xx3x	R/E	text	lg	lect/disc	test	none			01/03/98
87	15	07-07	TCH	SS	Recycling	3	x23x	R/E	mult	lg/ind	lect/ind	product	WWW/w proc/present/elec res, e-mail			01/03/98
86	10	11-12	CJC	LA	Catcher in the Rye	3	xx3x	I	mult	lg	lect/disc	report	none			09/27/97
68	20	11-12	BDE	SS	Supply and Demand	3	xx3x	I/R	mult	sg/lg	lect/disc	obs/swa	none			09/27/97
45	40	08-08	TMJ	Sci	Noise	2	x2xx	R-E	mult	sg/lg/ind	demo/disc	written report	WWW/w pro/present/elec res			09/27/97
20	10	10-10	MBE	Library	Web Authoring	9	x2xx	I	mult	ind	demo/prod/ind study	product (web page)	Front Page/HTML/scanner	5		09/27/97
17	15	10-12	RBW	Physics	Light	1	xx3x	I/R/E	text	lg	lect/disc	test	none			09/27/97
17	4	10-12	RBW	Physics	Light Lab	1	xx3x	I/R/E	laser, lab apparatus, text	lg - pairs	lect/lab	lab report	none			09/27/97
14	10	11-12	MAB	Spanish 4	Spanish Cooking	1	xxx4	E	mult	ind	ind	product	WWW			01/03/98

Integrating into the Curriculum: Curriculum Mapping
Sample Secondary Map — Sorted by Number of Students and Time

#STUD	TIME	GR	TCHR	SUBJ	UNIT	#SEC	MAR_PER	LEV	RES	ORG	METHODS	ASSIGN	TECH	Big6	SERV	DATE
120	2	05-05	MBE	Library	Biography	5	xx3x	R/E	mult	lg	lect/disc	none	online catalog	1 2 3	res prov	01/03/98
33	20	03-03	RDY	SS	Community	1	x2xx	R/E	mult	sg/lg	lect/disc/trip	project	Hyperstudio			01/03/98
33	15	03-03	RDY	Sci	Planets	1	xx3x	I	mult	sg/lg	lect/group	project	WWW			01/03/98
33	15	03-03	RDY	Sci	Endangered Animals	1	xxx4	I	mult	lg/ind	lect/disc/ind	project	Hyperstudio/WWW			01/03/98
32	10	01-01	MAB	Math	Whole/Parts	1	x2xx	I	text/mult	lg	lect/desk work	worksheet	none			01/03/98
29	40	06-06	SEW	SS	Current Events	1	1234	I/R/E	mult	lg/ind	disc/ind study	report	WWW			01/03/98
29	20	06-06	SEW	LA	Folktales and Legends	1	x23x	R/E	mult	lg	lect/disc/desk work	homework/ test	none			01/03/98
29	10	06-06	SEW	SS	Native Americans - Iroquois	1	x2xx	I	text	lg	lect/desk work	test	none			01/03/98
29	3	06-06	SEW	Sci	Vocabulary	1	1xxx	R/E	text	lg/ind	lect/desk work	homework	none			01/03/98
27	40	03-04	CAL	Sci	Simple Machines	1	1xxx	I/R	text/mult	sg	lab/ind study	products	none			09/27/97
27	15	03-04	CAL	Math	Graphs	1	xxx4	I	text	lg/ind	lect/desk work	product	none			09/27/97
27	8	03-04	CAL	LA	Letter Writing	1	x2xx	I	mult	ind	lect/desk work	product	w proc			09/27/97
27	8	03-04	CAL	Sci	Work and Energy	1	xxx4	I	text	lg	lect	text	none			09/27/97
25	15	01-01	REB	LA	ABC book	1	x2xx	R/E	mult	lg/ind	demo/ind study	product	none			01/03/98
24	40	00-00	LIE	LA	Colors	1	1234	I	mult	lg	disc/hands-on	worksheet	none			01/03/98

Planning an Integrated Program

Elementary School Example

Skills by Unit Matrix

The Big6: 1 Task Definition; 2 Information Seeking Strategies; 3 Location & Access; 4 Use of Information; 5 Synthesis; 6 Evaluation

GR	Tchr	Unit	Subject	Assignment	M_Per	1	2	3	4	5	6	Comments
00-00	LIE	Colors	LA	worksheet	1234	X	x	x	X	X	X	Introduce the Super3 and overall process.
01-01	REB	ABC book	LA	product	x2xx	X	x	x		X		Emphasize Task Definition and Synthesis.
01-01	MAB	Whole/Parts	Math	worksheet	x2xx				X		X	Use of worksheets.
03-03	RDY	Community	SS	project	x2xx	X	X	x	x		x	Determine and narrow - emphasize!
03-03	RDY	Planets	Sci	project	xx3x		X	X	x	X		Fun project, could use more time.
03-04	CAL	Simple Machines	Sci	products	1xxx	X				X		Different products.
03-04	CAL	Graphs	Math	product	xxx4				X	X		Presentation in different formats.
06-06	SEW	Current Events	SS	report	1234	X	X	X	X	X	X	All year long - can include all Big6.
06-06	SEW	Native Americans/Iroquois	SS	test	x2xx				X	X	X	Emphasize the output side of the process.

Planning an Integrated Program
Sample Skills by Unit Matrix: Middle School

Sorted by *grade level* and *marking period*

						The Big6						
GR	**Tchr**	**Unit**	**Subject**	**Assignment**	**QTR**	**1**	**2**	**3**	**4**	**5**	**6**	**Comments**
06-06	**SEW**	**Current Events**	**SS**	**report**	**1234**	**X**	**X**	**X**	**X**	**X**	**X**	All year long - can use all Big6.
06-06	**ARB**	**Poetry**	**English**	**short written assignment**	**xxx4**				**X**	**X**	**X**	#4 - reading poems, #5/6 - writing good poetry.
07-07	**SLJ**	**Graphs**	**Math**	**product**	**x2xx**				**X**	**X**		Types of graphs and spreadsheet software.
07-07	**TCH**	**Recycling**	**SS/Sci**	**product**	**x23x**	**-**	**X**	**X**	**-**	**X**	**-**	Lots of technology.
08-08	**HJW**	**Map Skills**	**SS**	**worksheet**	**1xxx**		**x**		**X**			Use of maps.
08-08	**TMJ**	**Noise**	**Sci**	**written report**	**x2xx**	**-**	**X**	**X**		**X**	**-**	Build on gr 7, technology.
07-08	**CER**	**Diet and Nutrition**	**Health**	**posters**	**1x3x**	**X**	**X**	**-**	**-**	**X**	**-**	Health reaches all students; repeats two times a year.
07-08	**CER**	**Tobacco and Smoking**	**Health**	**test**	**1x3x**	**X**			**X**	**X**	**X**	Cooperative teacher, test-taking strategies & the Big6.

Planning an Integrated Program

Secondary Example

Skills by Unit Matrix

The Big6: 1 Task Definition; 2 Information Seeking Strategies; 3 Location & Access; 4 Use of Information; 5 Synthesis; 6 Evaluation

GR	Tchr	Unit	Subject	Assignment	M_Per	1	2	3	4	5	6	Comments
07-07	TCH	Recycling	SS	product	x23x	X	X	X	x	X	x	Lots of technology.
08-08	HJW	Map Skills	SS	worksheet	1xxx		x		X			Use of maps.
08-08	TMJ	Noise	Sci	written report	x2xx	x	X	X		X	x	Build on gr 7, technology.
09-12	CER	Diet & Nutrition	Health	posters	1x3x	X	X	x	x	X	x	Health reaches all students; repeats two times a year.
09-12	CER	Tobacco and Smoking	Health	test	1x3x	X			X	X	X	Cooperative teacher, test-taking strategies and the Big6.
09-12	CER	Drugs	Health	product	x2x4	X	x	x	x	x	X	
11-12	CJC	Catcher in the Rye	LA	report	xx3x		X	X				Literary criticism resources.
11-12	BDE	Supply and Demand	SS	obs/swa	xx3x	X	X	X				First effort with this teacher.

Planning an Integrated Program
Sample Skills by Unit Matrix: Mr. Hancock - 4th Grade Teacher

					The Big6						
Unit	Subject	Assignment	M_Per	Pers	1	2	3	4	5	6	Comments
Spelling	Language Arts	Test	1234	40				X	.		*Strategies for learning/remembering spelling.*
State History	Social Studies	Written Report	12xx	30	X	X	X	X	X	X	*Major unit - lessons on all Big6.*
Geography	Social Studies	Maps, Product	1x3x	20	X				X		*Computer graphics to produce maps.*
Listening Skills	Language Arts	Test	1xxx	10	X			X			*Note-taking, tape recording.*
Personal Hygiene	Health	Ads, Product	1xxx	15	X	-			-	X	*Evaluating ads, creating posters.*
Letter Writing	Language Arts	Product	1xxx	15	X				X	X	*What makes a good letter? Using word processing.*
Food Groups	Health	Product (chart, posters, ads)	x2xx	15	X	X	X	X			*Periodical indexes on CD and the Web.*
Multiplication Tables-10s	Math	Test	x2xx	20				-			*Just mention ways to memorize.*
Structure of Plants	Science	Experiment, Test	xx34	20					X		*Lab reports - can computer generate.*
Rocks and Minerals	Science	Worksheet, Test	xx3x	20		X	X				*Use sources for worksheet - focus on determine, narrow, and keywords.*
Metric Measurements	Math	Test	xx3x	20		X	X				*Test will include examples of the metric system in action. Will need sources.*
Deserts/Life, Weather	Social Studies/Science	Written and Oral Report	xx3x	30	X	X	X				*Two subjects, lots of electronic Information Seeking Strategies, Location & Access.*
Mixed Numbers	Math	Worksheet	xx3x	20						X	*Self-evaluation.*

Planning an Integrated Program
Sample Skills by Unit Matrix: Social Studies Department

						The Big6						
GR	Tchr	Unit	Subject	Assignment	M_Per	1	2	3	4	5	6	Comments
9	Sullivan	Latin America	World History	Test	1xxx	X	-	-	-	X	X	*Test taking strategies - Task Definition, Synthesis.*
9	Sullivan	Northern Africa	World History	Test, Report	x2xx		X	X	X		-	*Sources - web searching, note-taking.*
9	Sullivan	India	World History	Maps, Product	xx3x					X		*Computer software to create various kinds of maps.*
10	Ryan	WW I	World History	Test	1xxx	X				X		
10	Ryan	Between the Wars	World History	Test, Short Written Assignment	12xx					X		*Essay writing strategies.*
10	Ryan	WW II	World History	Project, Test	x2xx		X	X	-	-		*Web-based information.*
10	Ryan	Cold War	World History	Test	xx3x						X	
10	Ryan	Vietnam	World History	Oral Report	xx34		-	-	X	X	-	*Presentation and graphics software.*
11	Rossini	Colonization of Western Hem.	World History	Test	1xxx	X			X			*Extracting relevant information from the textbook and notes.*
11	Rossini	Civil War	U.S. History	Report, Project	xx3x		X	X	X			*Using primary and secondary sources.*
11	Jackson	Constitution	U.S. History	Written and Oral Report	x2xx					X	X	*Presentation software (PowerPoint).*
11	Jackson	Civil War	U.S. History	Test	xx3x	X						*Nature of test.*
12	Petruso	Street Law	Government	Project	xxx4		X			X		*Community resources and law libraries.*
12	Valesky	Stock Market	Economics	Projext	1234	X	X	X	-	-	X	*Full-year, competitive intelligence.*

Planning an Integrated Program

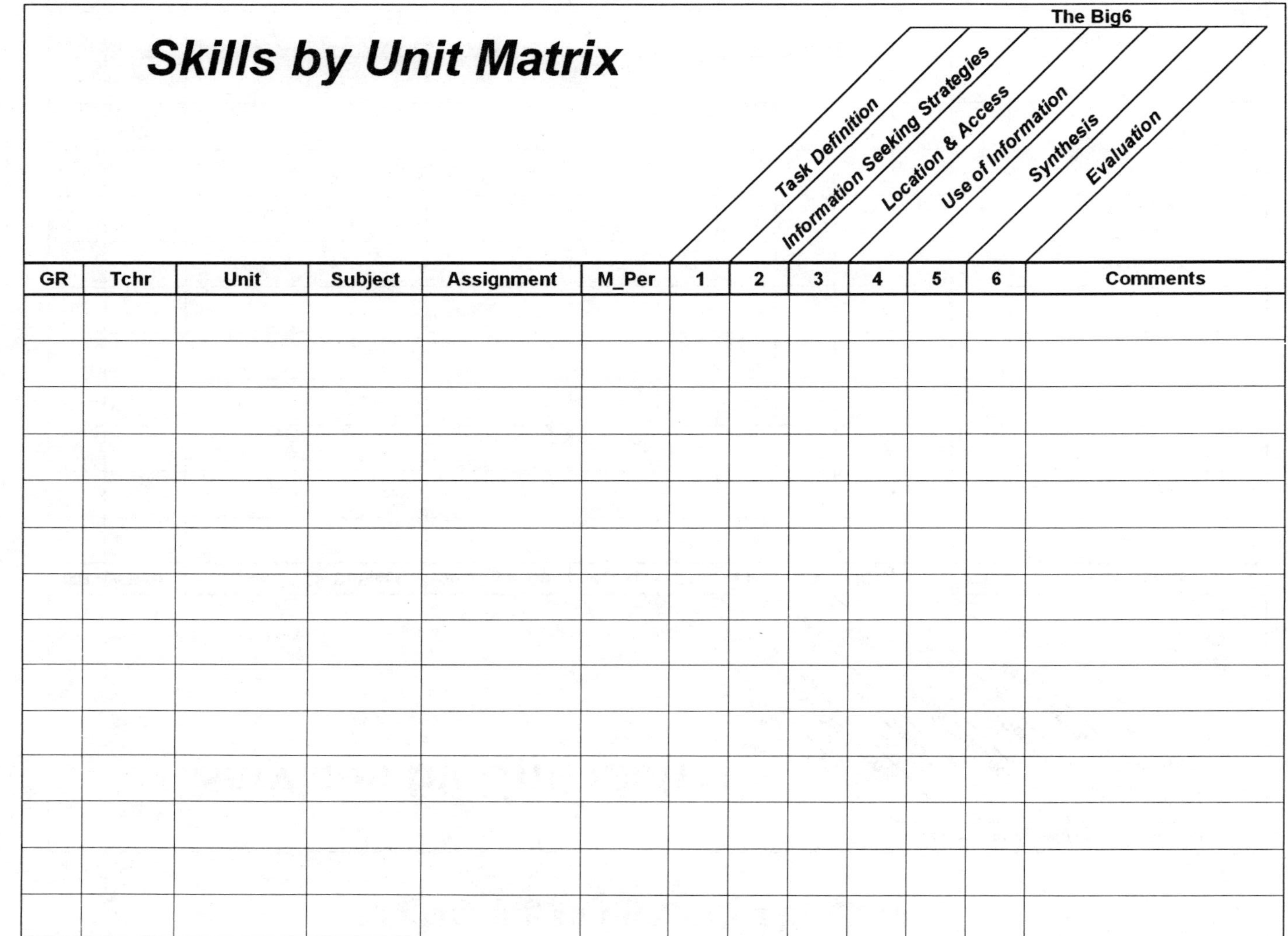

Skills by Unit Matrix

						The Big6						
						Task Definition	Information Seeking Strategies	Location & Access	Use of Information	Synthesis	Evaluation	
GR	Tchr	Unit	Subject	Assignment	M_Per	1	2	3	4	5	6	Comments

Planning an Integrated Program

Services by Unit Matrix

Information, Library, and Technology Services

Resources Provision
Facilities Provision
Reading/Media Guidance
Information Service
Skills Instruction
Info/Curriculum Consultation

GR	Tchr	Unit	Subject	Assignment	M_Per	RP	FP	RG	IS	SI	ICC	Comments

Planning an Integrated Program
Big6 Curriculum — Year Timeline Planner (K-12)

GR	Tchr	Subject	Assignment	1 3 5 7 9 11 13 15 17 19 21 23 25 27 29 31 33 35 37 39	1	2	3	4	5	6
00-00	LIE	LA	worksheet	******************************COLORS******************************	x	x	x	x	x	x
01-01	REB	LA	product		x	x	x		x	
01-01	MAB	Math	worksheet	ABC Book				x		x
03-03	RDY	SS	project	COMMUNITY****	x	x	x	x		x
03-03	RDY	Sci	project	**PLANETS**		x	x	x	x	
03-04	CAL	Sci	products	SIMPLE MACHINES******	x				x	
03-04	CAL	Math	product	GRAPHS				x	x	
06-06	SEW	SS	report	******************************Current Events******************************	x	x	x	x	x	x
06-06	SEW	SS	test	IROQUOIS****				x	x	x
07-07	TCH	SS	product	RECYCLING	x	x	x	x	x	x
08-08	HJW	SS	worksheet	Map Skills		x		x		
08-08	TMJ	Sci	wr report	NOISE******************************	x	x	x		x	x
09-12	CER	Health	posters	Diet/Nuitrition; Diet/Nuitrition	x	x	x	x	x	x
09-12	CER	Health	test	Smoking; Smoking	x			x	x	x
09-12	CER	Health	product	DRUGS**; DRUGS**	x	x	x	x	x	x
11-12	CJC	LA	report	Catcher/Rye		x	x			
11-12	BDE	SS	obs/swa	Supply and Demand**	x	x	x			

Planning an Integrated Program
Big6 Curriculum — Year Timeline Planner (K-12)

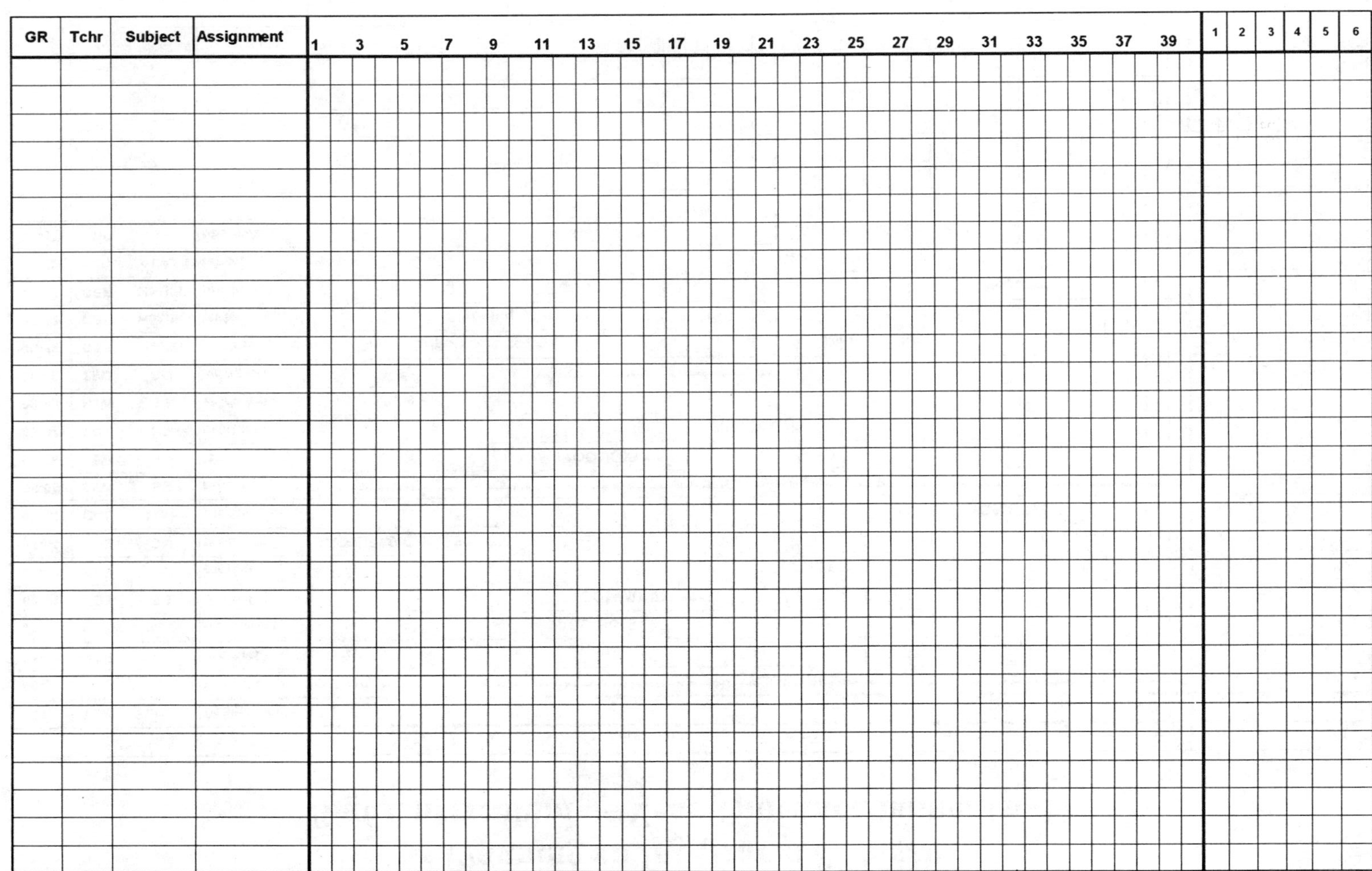

GR	Tchr	Subject	Assignment	1		3		5		7		9		11		13		15		17		19		21		23		25		27		29		31		33		35		37		39		1	2	3	4	5	6

Think Sheet

Part VIII:

The Parent Connection

Introduction

This Part of the *Workshop Handbook* focuses on the parent or caregiver connection. Parents and caregivers can be important partners for educators in helping students to gain information skills and to succeed in school. We often hold parent/community workshops and sessions to encourage parents to get involved and to do so in constructive and meaningful ways. We find that parents are eager audiences and we encourage using the materials in this section (as well as our *Helping With Homework* book) to conduct your own parent/community sessions.

These sessions do not need to be long—one hour maximum or even as short as 15-20 minutes. The point is to help parents understand the Big6 themselves and then learn to guide their children through assignments and tasks using the Big6. Our sessions usually take the following outline:

- The information age: Implications for learning & teaching
- Information literacy: The Big6 Skills process & approach
- The parent role
- The technology connection
- Q&A.

The materials in this Part of the Workshop Handbook are also designed for use in parent/community sessions.

The "Overview" slides are used to explain the parent role. We emphasize that parents can help and use the Big6 at three different points in time:

- Before their children actually start their homework—by talking the students through the process
- During the work—by troubleshooting with their children if they get stuck
- After their children are finished—by checking their work.

The detailed chart, "Helping With Homework," provides three different examples of guiding and coaching. We find it really helps adult audiences to understand how to use the Big6 to guide students.

Two exercises are provided to further develop guiding and coaching skills. One exercise deals with a single assignment (the astronomy paper) while the other offers scenarios from a variety of situations. We sometimes break parent/community audiences into groups, work through the exercises, and then discuss with the full audience.

The "Hopsicker Letter" is an example of communication from a teacher to parents explaining the information skills—classroom connection. The "Helping With Homework: A Big6 Assignment Organizer" is a useful tool for helping students to stay on top of their assignments.

Lastly, the ERIC Digest, "Helping With Homework: A Parent's Guide to Information Problem-Solving," brings it all together. The digest can be copied and distributed at presentations.

Parents and caregivers can and should play an important role in helping their children succeed. However, while well-intentioned in providing assistance, parents often lack the necessary understandings and approaches to truly help. In fact, many times, parent-children help sessions wind up in conflict and confrontation.

We encourage parents to avoid confrontation by using the Big6 to help guide or coach. With the Big6, parents are not being asked to teach—as that usually leads to their children exclaiming "that's not the way my teacher does it!" Rather, the parents are guiding their children on teacher-determined, established goals and curriculum.

Overview
Information & Technology Skills for Student Success: The Big6™ Skills Approach

The Parent Connection: Helping with Homework

"Parents can make a difference by helping, not by teaching or doing."

- from *Helping with Homework, 1997*

Parents can assist children to learn how to approach information problems (both in and out of school) and to choose the tools to solve those problems.

Approach for Parents

- Parent as helper-guide
  - before homework: talk through
  - during homework: troubleshoot
  - after homework: check
- Using the Big6 Process
  - a tool for solving information problems
  - context for use of technology

Eisenberg & Berkowitz, 1988

Helping With Homework
Information Problem-Solving in School, Life, and Work Contexts

Information Problem-Solving Process	1st Grade Language Arts - Maria's homework is to make an ABC book.	7th Grade Social Studies - Leon has to do a social studies report (three minute oral with visual aids) on recycling.	10th Grade Math - Joanne is working on probability homework problems. She missed two days of school this week.
Task Definition	After the teacher explains the assignment, Maria decides that she will make an ABC book based on the topic of food. In talking with her mother, she realizes she will need to gather lots of foods (and spellings).	Leon decides to narrow the topic of recycling to investigate ways of recycling tires.	Joanne realizes that because she missed school, she doesn't really know how to do the problems assigned.
Information Seeking Strategies	Maria decides to ask her mother for help in getting information about foods. Together they realize that a cookbook might help and that maybe she can find one for kids in the library media center.	Leon talks to the school library media specialist about his idea. She suggests using CD-ROM magazine indexes and searching the World Wide Web as two good sources.	Joanne asks her older brother what she should do. He asks what the teacher relies on most - the textbook or class notes. Joanne says that class notes are most important.
Location & Access	The library media specialist helps Maria to find a children's cookbook.	Leon searches using the Magazine Articles Summaries CD-ROM and also searches the WWW using *Yahoo*.	Joanne calls her friend Tonya and arranges to go over to her house to look at her notes.
Information Use	Maria reads through the book to find the names of fruits, vegetables, and other foods. She writes each name on a card.	Leon reads the articles on the screen and is able to cut and paste directly into his word processor.	Tonya explains how the notes are organized and shows Joanne the pages that specifically relate to the homework. Joanne copies Tonya's notes.
Synthesis	Maria uses pictures from magazines, construction paper, and crayons to illustrate her book. She puts all the pages in alphabetical order and staples them together. Maria practices reading her ABC book to her mother.	He practices his presentation. He makes a few changes in order to be more specific about the benefits of recycling tires.	Joanne is able to do three of the problems, but gets stuck on the other three. She writes a note on her homework that she needs additional help.
Evaluation	Maria decides that she likes her book, but that coming up with an idea for the letter "X" was hard.	Leon reviews his draft and realizes he has plenty of specific information on recycling tires but needs to add more general information about recycling in the introduction.	Joanne realizes that she still needs direct information from her teacher and arranges to come in for extra help.

Parent Exercise
Big6™ Skills: Developing an Understanding in Context

Parent Exercise: The Astronomy Paper. Your child is studying astronomy. The assignment is to write a paper about a trip to a planet or other body in the solar system. Please try to identify the relevant Big6 stage and note possible actions that you might take. Note: There are six situations, one for each Big6.

Situations	Big6	Your Possible Actions
Your child says, "I can't find anything on Mars. How am I supposed to do this project anyway?"		
Your child is confused about exactly what to do and asks, "Isn't this just a typical astronomy report?" What do you do?		
Your child is having trouble creating a picture using a paint program. What can you do?		
Your child is having trouble reading from your neighbor's college astronomy textbook. How can you help?		
Your child asks you to check to see if all necessary parts are included. What do you do?		
Your child is having trouble finding information on Callisto in the encyclopedia. How can you help?		

The Big6 Skills © 1987 Eisenberg & Berkowitz

Task Definition

1.1 Define the problem.

1.2 Identify the information needed.

Information Seeking Strategies

2.1 Determine all possible sources.

2.2 Select the best sources.

Location & Access

3.1 Locate sources.

3.2 Find information within sources.

Use of Information

4.1 Engage (e.g., read, hear, view).

4.2 Extract relevant information.

Synthesis

5.1 Organize info from multiple sources.

5.2 Present the result.

Evaluation

6.1 Judge the result (effectiveness).

6.2 Judge the process (efficiency).

Parent Exercise
Big6™ Skills: Developing an Understanding in Context

General Exercise: Parent-Student Interactions. Below are examples of problems that students might have in a variety of situations. Please try to identify the relevant Big6 Skill and note possible actions that you might take. Note: More than one Big6 may apply to a given situation and not all Big6 are necessarily used.

Situations	Big6	Your Possible Actions
Your 11th grade daughter is flipping through a thick guide to colleges. She's frustrated and anxious and says, "Maybe I just won't go to college."		
Your son is working on a 4th grade science experiment. He asks for help because he doesn't know how he should take notes on his observations.		
Your daughter and her friend complain that they doesn't know what's on tomorrow's test.		
Your son just finished his literary criticism paper. You ask, "How did you do?" He responds, "I haven't a clue."		
You rush in the room after your daughter screams, "I just can't do this!" You see her staring a the shoebox full of notecards for her geography report.		
Calvin says, "If I had a computer, I'm sure I'd get better grades on my book reports."		

The Big6 Skills © 1987 Eisenberg & Berkowitz

Task Definition

1.1 Define the problem.

1.2 Identify the information needed.

Information Seeking Strategies

2.1 Determine all possible sources.

2.2 Select the best sources.

Location & Access

3.1 Locate sources.

3.2 Find information within sources.

Use of Information

4.1 Engage (e.g., read, hear, view).

4.2 Extract relevant information.

Synthesis

5.1 Organize info from multiple sources.

5.2 Present the result.

Evaluation

6.1 Judge the result (effectiveness).

6.2 Judge the process (efficiency).

SAMPLE **SAMPLE** **SAMPLE** **SAMPLE** **SAMPLE**

Mr. Scott Hopsicker
Wayne Central High School
Social Studies Department

October 8, 1997

Dear Parent or Guardian,

As a teacher, and more importantly your student's Social Studies teacher, I know that parents/guardians can be key partners in helping their children be successful in school. I am asking for your help because parents/guardians can provide an atmosphere which fosters achievement and success. However, the question is, "What can parents/guardians do to help their students that will have the biggest impact?" Answer: Assignments—especially homework.

U.S. History and Government is designed to be a conceptual course aimed at giving students an understanding of events and issues that impact social, political, economic and foreign policy concerns. The course covers such topics as: the constitution, impact of the presidents, and supreme court cases throughout America's history. Homework is assigned on a regular basis. Assignments are ways for my students to show me what they know. They are also ways for students to learn, review, remediate, or extend what is taught in my classroom. To be successful on quizzes and tests in this course, the homework must be done.

You can help your student be successful with their homework assignments by guiding, assisting, and generally making it easier for them to succeed. The attached "Homework Planner" offers a framework that you can use to guide students through assignments and homework. I think that this simple tool can make a big difference. I will make copies available for all students and encourage that they be used to help organize homework assignments. I hope you will help me by using this organizer with your student whenever he/she has homework in U.S. History and Government.

Please feel free to contact me at the high school whenever you have any concerns. If you leave a message at the main office, I will return your call as soon as possible.

Thank you in advance for your support and cooperation.

Sincerely,

Scott Hopsicker

Reprinted with author's permission.

SAMPLE **SAMPLE** **SAMPLE** **SAMPLE** **SAMPLE**

Helping With Homework
A Big6™ Assignment Organizer

Assignment: ________________________________ **Date Due:** ____________

Complete Big6 Skills #1-5 BEFORE you BEGIN your assignment.
Complete Big6 Skill #6 BEFORE you TURN IN your assignment.

Big6 Skill #1: Task Definition

What does this assignment require me to do?

What information do I need in order to do this assignment?

Big6 Skill #2: Information Seeking Strategies

What sources can I use to do the assignment?
Circle the best sources.

Big6 Skill #3: Location & Access

Where can I find my sources? Do I need help?
If so, who can help me?

Big6 Skill #4: Use of Information

What do I have to do with the information?

_____ read/view/listen
_____ take notes
_____ answer questions
_____ other: ____________________

_____ chart and/or write an essay
_____ copy and highlight
_____ properly cite

Big6 Skill #5: Synthesis

What product does this assignment require?

Big6 Skill #6: Evaluation

Student self-evaluation checklist:

_____ I did what I was supposed to do (see Big6 #1, Task Definition)
_____ The assignment is complete.

The Big6 Eisenberg & Berkowitz, 1987. Assignment Organizer © Berkowitz & Hopsicker, 1997.

November 1996 EDO-IR-96-09

Helping With Homework: A Parent's Guide to Information Problem-Solving

by Robert E. Berkowitz

This Digest is based on the book, Helping With Homework: A Parent's Guide to Information Problem-Solving, by Michael B. Eisenberg & Robert E. Berkowitz

Introduction

Parents can play an important role in helping their children succeed in school, but they need an effective approach in order to do this well. The approach taken in the book, *Helping with Homework: A Parent's Guide to Information Problem-Solving*, is based on the Big Six Skills problem-solving approach. The Big Six Skills apply to any problem or activity that requires a solution or result based on information. An abundance of information is available from many sources, and the Big Six can help parents effectively deal with that information to guide their youngsters through school assignments.

The Big Six Approach

The Big Six approach has six components: task definition, information seeking strategies, location and access, use of information, synthesis, and evaluation.

- Task Definition: In the task definition stage, students need to determine what is expected from the assignment.
- Information Seeking Strategies: Once students know what's expected of them, they need to identify the resources they will need to solve the task as defined. This is information seeking.
- Location & Access: Next, the students must find potentially useful resources. This is location and access—the implementation of the information seeking strategy.
- Use of Information: Use of information requires the students to engage the information (e.g., read it) and decide how to use it (e.g., in text or in a footnote).
- Synthesis: Synthesis requires the students to repackage the information to meet the requirements of the task as defined.
- Evaluation: Finally, students need to evaluate their work on two levels before it is turned in to the teacher. Students need to know if their work will meet their teacher's expectations for (1) quality and (2) efficiency.

The Big Six steps may be applied in any order, but all steps must be completed.

Parents' Role and Students' Role

The Big Six approach requires parents and students to assume different roles. The parent assumes the role of a "coach" and the child assumes the role of "thinker and doer." As a coach, the parent can use the Big Six Skills to guide the student through all the steps it takes to complete the assignment. Parents can help by first asking their children to explain assignments in their own words. This is "task definition"—a logical first step. Parents can also help by discussing possible sources of information. This is "information seeking strategies." Parents can then help their children implement information seeking strategies by helping their children find useful resources. This is the Big Six step called "location and access." Location and access may have to be repeated during an assignment because some children may not identify everything they need right at the beginning. Parents can facilitate by brainstorming with their children alternate places where information might be available. In the "use of information" stage, parents can discuss whether the information the child located is relevant and if so, help the child decide how to use it. In the "synthesis" stage, parents can ask for a summary of the information in the child's own words, and ask whether the information meets the requirements identified in the "task definition" stage. The end of any assignment is the final check‹an evaluation of all the work that has been done. Parents can help their children with the "evaluation" stage by discussing whether the product answers the original question, whether it meets the teacher's expectations, and whether the project could have been done more efficiently.

As children work through each of the Big Six steps, they need to think about what they need to do, and then they need to find appropriate ways to do it. This is their role— "thinker and doer." Children should be encouraged to be as independent as possible, but they will often have difficulty beginning an assignment because they are confused about what is expected of them. Whatever the reason is for their inability to get started, students have the ultimate responsibility for getting their work done. When parents act as coaches, they can help their children assume this responsibility by engaging them in conversation about what is expected of them, and then by guiding them throughout the assignment using the Big Six Skills.

Why Assignments?

Assignments provide students with an opportunity to review and practice new material, to correct errors in understanding and production, and to assess levels of mastery. Every assignment is an information problem that can be solved using the Big Six. For instance, the goal of many assignments is to have the students practice a skill taught in class. If a child is having a problem understanding an assignment, the parent may help by encouraging the child to explain what it is he or she does not understand. The parent can use information seeking strategies to help the child identify information sources by asking questions such as: "Is there another student in your class, who can help you understand how to do this?" or, "Did the teacher give any other examples?" The parent can help the child identify information sources and suggest ways to get them. For instance, the public television network may have a homework hotline, the public library may have study guides, or a neighborhood child may be in the same class.

Technology and The Big Six

The Big Six approach recognizes the benefits of technology in education because computers are tools that help organize information. Software programs do a variety of functions such as edit written work, check grammar and spelling, chart and graph quantities, and construct outlines. Computers can also help with time management, setting priorities, and evaluating efficiency.

Using the Internet, students can connect to many non-traditional sources of information and are not limited to information contained on library shelves. They can use e-mail to talk directly with specialists and experts who can add a personal dimension to an assignment.

Conclusion

It is an axiom of American education that parents are partners in their children's education. Parents have traditionally participated by helping their children with homework. The Big Six approach can help parents effectively guide their children through assignments and at the same time help their children become independent learners and users of information.

Bibliography

Eisenberg, M. B. & Berkowitz, R. E. (1990). *Information problem solving: The Big Six Skills approach to library and information skills instruction.* Norwood, NJ: Ablex. Ablex Publishing Corporation, 355 Chestnut St. Norwood, NJ 07648 ($22.95). Document not available from EDRS. (ED 330 364)

Eisenberg, M. B. & Berkowitz, R. E. (1992). Information problem-solving: The Big Six Skills approach. *School Library Media Activities Monthly, 8*(5), 27-29,37,42. (EJ 438 023)

Eisenberg, M. B. & Berkowitz, R. E. (1995, August). The six study habits of highly effective students: Using the Big Six to link parents, students, and homework. *School Library Journal, 41*(8), 22-25. (EJ 510 346)

Eisenberg, M. B. & Spitzer, K. L. (1991, Oct.) Skills and strategies for helping students become more effective information users. *Catholic Library World, 63*(2), 115-120. (EJ 465 828)

Granowsky, A. (1991). What parents can do to help children succeed in school. *PTA Today, 17*(1), 5-6. (EJ 436 757)

Indiana State Department of Education. (1990). *Get ready, get set, parent's role: Parent booklet.* [Booklet]. Indianapolis, IN: Author. (ED 337 264)

Konecki, L. R. (1992). *Parent talk: Helping families relate to schools and facilitate children's learning.* Paper presented at the Annual Meeting of the Association of Teacher Educators (Orlando, FL, February 17, 1992). (ED 342 745)

Lankes, R. D. (1996). *The bread & butter of the Internet: A primer and presentation packet for educators.* (IR-101). Syracuse, NY: ERIC Clearinghouse on Information & Technology. (ED number pending)

Scarnati, J. T. & Platt, R. B. (1991, Oct.) Lines and pies and bars, oh my! Making math fun. *PTA Today, 17*(1), 9-11. (EJ 436 759)

Van, J. A. (1991, Oct.). Parents are part of the team at Hearst Award Winner's school. *PTA Today, 17*(1), 7-8. (EJ 436 758)

This ERIC Digest was prepared by Robert E. Berkowitz, K-12 coordinator of library programs at Wayne Central School District in Ontario Center, NY, and adjunct instructor at Syracuse University's School of Information Studies.

ERIC Digests are in the public domain and may be freely reproduced and disseminated.

ERIC Clearinghouse on Information & Technology, 4-194 Center for Science and Technology, Syracuse University, Syracuse, NY 13244-4100; (315) 443-3640; Fax: (315) 443-5448; e-mail: eric@ericir.syr.edu; or URL: http://ericir.syr.edu/ithome

This publication was prepared with funding from the Office of Educational Research and Improvement, U.S. Department of Education, under contract no. RR93002009. The opinions expressed in this report do not necessarily reflect the positions of OERI or ED.

ERIC Clearinghouse on Information & Technology Syracuse University • 4-194
Center for Science and Technology • Syracuse, NY 13244-4100 • 800-464-9107 • http://ericir.syr.edu/ithome

Parents: Help your children achieve

Guide them through homework assignments using the Big Six© problem-solving approach

- **"Our goal is simple but powerful: to give parents an effective approach and the tools they need to help their children learn and achieve."—Eisenberg and Berkowitz**

Helping With Homework: A Parent's Guide to Information Problem-Solving

by Michael B. Eisenberg and Robert E. Berkowitz

Michael B. Eisenberg
is professor of Information Studies at Syracuse University, director of the ERIC Clearinghouse on Information & Technology, author, and co-founder of AskERIC.

Robert E. Berkowitz
is library media specialist at Wayne Central High School, adjunct professor at Syracuse University's School of Information Studies, author and consultant.

This handbook shows parents a tested approach for helping children of all ages learn and achieve in an information society. By applying the Big Six© Skills for information problem-solving model, parents can help students fully understand and successfully complete homework and other school tasks.

Eisenberg and Berkowitz apply the Big Six© model to sample assignments in language arts, science, math, social studies, as well as to real life situations. The authors also discuss the benefits of using computer software and hardware, the Internet, and other educational technology tools as part of the information problem-solving process.

Eisenberg/Berkowitz
Helping with Homework
A Parent's Guide to Information Problem-Solving

182 pp., 6"x9", IR-102; $20.00 plus $3. shipping. (ISBN: 0-937597-42-2)

Check out these other new ERIC/IT resources!

AskA Starter Kit: How to Build and Maintain Digital Reference Services

by R. David Lankes and Abby S. Kasowitz

This set of six self-instructional modules prepares organizations and indi-viduals to create an Internet-based human-mediated information service. Real-life experiences from existing digital reference services like AskERIC, the National Museum of American Art Reference Desk, NASA's Ask the Space Scientist, KidsConnect, and Ask Dr. Math provide helpful hints for new services. Modules include: Informing: Gather information; Planning: Develop an AskA Plan; Training: Prepare training programs; Prototyping: Pilot test the AskA service; Contributing: Promote the service and Go Live!; Evaluating: Assess service quality. **235 pp., 8.5" x 11"; IR-107; spiral; $20.00 plus $3. shipping. (ISBN: 0-937597-47-3)**

Survey of Instructional Development Models

Third Edition

by Kent L. Gustafson and Robert Maribe Branch

This popular text, now in its third edition, presents a brief history of instructional development (ID) models and describes how ID models influence the process of teaching and learning. These instructional development models serve as tools for:

- analyzing
- designing
- creating, and
- evaluating guided learning.

Gustafson and Branch select and describe models that are representative of ID literature and that reflect the main concepts found in most other ID models. The authors evaluate and discuss ID models that are useful for classroom, product, or system orientations. Illustrations of each ID model are included. **106 pp., 6" x 9"; IR-103; spiral; $20.00 plus $3. shipping. (ISBN: 0-937597-43-0)**

Information Literacy: Essential Skills for the Information Age

by Kathleen L. Spitzer with Michael B. Eisenberg and Carrie Lowe

This monograph traces the history and development of the term information literacy, examines the economic necessity of being information literate, and explores the research related to the concept. The book reports on the National Educational Goals (1991) and the Secretary's Commission on Achieving Necessary Skills (SCANS) Report (1991).

The authors examine recent revisions in national subject matter standards that imply a recognition of the process skills included in information literacy and outline the impact of information literacy on K–12 and higher education.

Finally, the book provides examples of information literacy in various contexts. An extensive ERIC bibliography is appended. **377 pp., 6" x 9"; IR-104; $18.00 plus $3. shipping. (ISBN: 0-937597-44-9)**

Order Form

Order no.	Qty.	Title	Price	Total
IR-102		Helping With Homework	$20.00	
IR-107		AKA Starter Kit: How to Build and Maintain Digital Reference Services	$20.00	
IR-103		Survey of Instructional Development Models	$20.00	
IR-104		Information Literacy: Essential Skills for the Information Age	$18.00	

Your satisfaction is guaranteed.

If for any reason you are not totally satisfied with a product or publication you purchase from ERIC/IT, you may return the item within 30 days, and we will refund your money.

*** Shipping and Handling:**

If your order is:	Your S&H charge is:
$0.00 -$30.00	$3.00
$31.00-$500.00	10% of order
over $500.00	7% of order

Subtotal ______
Shipping & Handling ______
TOTAL ______

(1) To order:

Mail: ***ERIC Clearinghouse on Information & Technology***
Syracuse University
4-194 Center for Science and Technology
Syracuse, New York 13244-4100
Telephone: 800-464-9107
E-mail: eric@ericir.syr.edu

(2) Method of payment:

Make checks payable to:
Information Resources Publications, or
Please ship immediately and bill my Purchase Order Number: #________________. Terms net 30.

(3) Ship to:

Name ________________
Title ________________
Organization ________________
Address ________________

(4) Bill to:

Name ________________
Title ________________
Organization ________________
Address ________________

Think Sheet

Part IX:

Closing

Introduction

After working through the worksheets, exercises, and readings in this *Handbook*, you should be well-informed about the Big6 process and approach. You should also have some conceptual frameworks and practical methods for planning and implementing Big6 Skills instruction on the district, school, and classroom level.

The Big6 is an approach to information and technology skills instruction that puts students in a position to be successful information problem-solvers. In the *Handbook*, we emphasized:

- The nature and scope of the Big6 Skills
- The purpose and use of curriculum maps for planning integrated curriculum
- Needs and mechanisms for instructional design and planning on the macro and micro levels
- The role of assessment in terms of efficiency and effectiveness
- Collaborative roles for all educators as well as parents, community members, and even students in implementing meaningful Big6 instruction.

What remains is to look ahead and more formally plan for the future; to take all of these parts and forge them into a cohesive whole. This requires:

- Assessing the current status of your own level of expertise as well as the status of integrated skills instruction at the school or district level
- Determining what is desirable in terms of meeting students' needs to attain Big6 Skills
- Determining what it will take in terms of curriculum, technology, and planning to meet students needs
- Establishing a timeframe for accomplishing these goals.

In this Part, we provide forms and charts to begin this kind of long-term planning for effective Big6 Skills instruction. These tools will help to analyze students' needs as well as the status of personal, school, and district inputs. They provide a mechanism to gauge the extent of your own expertise, the needs of students, and the current degree of the school community's cooperation. You can then use this base to plan for further personal and systemic development.

We urge you to "think big!" Information and technology skills instruction is not optional; it's not an add-on. Big6 Skills instruction is part of a basic skills education in the 21st century.

To borrow from the mission statement of the American Association of School Librarians and the Association for Educational Communications and Technology, our goal is "to ensure that students are effective users of ideas and information" (*Information Power*, 1988, p. 1; 1998, p. 6).

We are confident that you will use the ideas, strategies, and tools offered in this handbook to make a difference in your schools and communities. We encourage you to customize and personalize the various forms and activities in order to envision, analyze, plan, implement, and evaluate on your own.

Again—think Big(6)!

Personal Planning

	Current Status	Needs	Time Frame
Curriculum: Instructional Design			
Big6 Information and Technology Skills			
Technology: Personal Skills			
Technology: Context			
Planning: Micro			
Planning: Macro			

School or District Planning

	Current Status	Needs	Time Frame
Student Skills and Needs			
Curriculum			
Big6 Information and Technology Skills Instruction			
Technology			
Planning: Macro			

Assessment: Big6™—Big View

1. Determine key **indicators** for a quality Big6 program.
2. Review the **current status** for each indicator.
3. **Comment** to help guide action planning.

Indicator	Current Status	Comment
Example: • Big6 Skills are integrated throughout the curriculum.	Example: • There is a Long Range Curriculum Planning Team that includes classroom teachers, library media specialist, and technology teacher. • An analysis of the Curriculum Map shows Big6 "Bonanza" units in science, social studies, and language arts—grades 6 and 8. Also, strong Big6 units in science and health—grade 7.	Example: • Need to develop or redesign units in art, music, and math—grades 6 through 8.

Big6™ Program Planning Worksheet

	Immediate	Short Term	Long Term
What do I want to have happen?			
How can I make it happen?			
Who can help me and how can they help?			
What will I accept as evidence that I am achieving my goals?			
What will I do tomorrow?			

Putting it all Together
Information & Technology Skills for Student Success: The Big6™ Skills Approach

Final Suggestions

- Recognize the dilemmas of the information age
- Accept the "Technology and Internet Challenge"
- Remember context #1: The information problem-solving process (the Big6)
- Remember context #2: The curriculum and real needs
- Collaborate: Classroom teachers, administrators, library media specialists, students, community
- Think BIG — this is important stuff!!

Think Sheet

Big6 Session Participant Evaluation—Let Us Know What You Think!

Big6 Session Location: Date:

Concerning the Big6 Session:

1. Please explain your reasons and goals for attending.

2. Please explain to what degree the session met your goals and expectations.

3. What worked particularly well?

4. What would you suggest to improve the session?

5. If you were to attend another session on the Big6, what do you think it should include?

Concerning Future Big6 Materials:

Due to popular demand, we are working on additional support materials that will help you teach the Big6 Skills. We would appreciate your input. Would you take a moment to answer a few questions?

1. Would you like Big6 materials to use with students? If so, what kinds of materials?

2. Would you like Big6 materials to use with teachers, other faculty, or parents? If so, what kinds of materials?

3. Would you like Big6 examples for each curriculum?

4. Do you have Big6 lessons or units that you have developed? Would you be willing to share them?

5. What other kinds of Big6 materials would be useful to you?

6. Would you like to hear about new Big6 materials as soon as they become available? If so, please complete the following:

   Name:
   Title:
   School:
   Address:
   City, State, Zip:

   Phone:
   e-mail:
   Alternative address to send information:

Thanks!!
Mike & Bob

Marlene Woo-Lun
Linworth Publishing, Inc.
480 E. Wilson Bridge Road, Ste. L
Worthington, OH 43085

NORTHERN MICHIGAN UNIVERSITY
3 1854 006 801 214